MW01075434

Roadmap to Radiance

A memoir

Camden Hoch

Rick,
You are a light of radiance and good in the world! Happy adventures abound!
Love,
Camden

Copyright © 2016 Camden Hoch

All rights reserved.

ISBN: 1533502617
ISBN-13: 978-1533502612

For my beautiful, strong, and courageous daughters, Lily and Emma, and my loving, amazing husband, Luke. I love you.

Contents

Acknowledgments

Writing this book about my life awakened a fresh vulnerability through which I see more clearly what truly matters and I'm acting on it every day. Love is all that matters and is always the solution. Acceptance is the road to love. Always. I fully accept and love myself as I am.

Lily and Emma. These girls. These girls teach me courage, strength, and power. They teach me beauty and love. They do it by being themselves and allowing me to learn, grow, love, take risks, and live more adventures in life. I give thanks for being a mom.

I give thanks for being a wife to Luke. Since we met, Luke's grounding presence has inspired me to trust being myself and stand in the power of my true voice. Luke, Lily, and Emma are my grounding and rooting forces who inspire me to rise, spread my wings, and soar. Thank you, my loves, for holding the space and encouraging me to write, cry, laugh, and live the creative expression of my heart with you.

I am grateful to my parents, Lib and Frank, for bringing me into this life and loving me. Without them, I would not be here now on the mission that I'm inspired and Divinely propelled to share with the world. Thank you Dad for believing in me and being there in my bravest and lowest moments and all the in between times. Thank you Mom for accepting and loving me as I am and understanding I have my own path to lead. We've come a long way. I love you.

I am thankful to my brother who was always there with me when we were young, even though we weren't so close in age or in school. We always have known that we can be there for each other.

I'm thankful for my grandparents, Nannie and Paw Paw, Neno and Grandaddy, for their stable, fun and nurturing roles in my life. I miss them but can still feel their loving strong presence in my life.

With so many words and so many memories flooding the pages as I wrote, when I questioned the process of how it would all coagulate to form a book that others would be led to read, my publisher extraordinaire, Kim Eldredge of New Frontier Books told me to keep writing from my heart. She has been there every step of the way encouraging me and providing a structure for the publication process. Thank you Kim for listening, guiding, and helping me produce a book that is real and inspires others to let go of anything keeping them in a holding pattern so they can dive into the adventures everyday in their lives and stand in the power of their true voice.

I am grateful to my coaches for holding me in a safe container as I dug into past pain, reminding me of the present so I wouldn't get lost again in the running and addictions. We are not meant to walk alone.

I am grateful for the water in all forms in my life and it's great reminder that there is a greater beingness in my life. God guides me from within to live new adventures, to put myself out there and to share my story in inspirations for others to create the lives they were meant to live.

I am grateful to all the teachers I've met on the road; all of my experiences and all of the people I've known who have influenced my path and arrival at where I am today. I am so humbly privileged to call yoga my spiritual practice and to recognize all of the gifts and clarity from my practice. I am in my body, integrated, and so full of thankfulness for this journey. Life is whole, filled with crazy adventures, and even though the ride can still be up and down, I don't crash anymore. I am grateful for wholeness and the love that has expanded in my life. I am happy to live it and pass it on for others to join the adventure.

I am grateful to the yoga teachers who have and continue to influence my life in thought provoking and positive ways - Sabine Vera, Shri Hamilton Hubbard, Stan Hubbard, Baron Baptiste, Sarah Powers, Janet Stone, Rusty Wells, Stephanie Keach, and Tias Little.

I am grateful to my friend Annette, who walks and talks with me. Thank you, sister, for always being there.

My friend Peter who helped me see more love and trust through the light of our friendship.

My friends Richard and Josh who are my family. We will always have the "mouse house" memories in our heart and I am so thankful for your love and always the laughter, laundry, and pasta with peas.

Thank you to Joanna, Julie, Linda, David, Mary Lou, Mark, Stacey, Rena, Traci, Helen, Rema, Cardin, Rebecca, Karen, Joanne, Re, Joe, Justin, Gail, Michele, Greg, Giovanna, Barbara, Nance, Deborah, Mickie, Francis, Shelley, Kelley, Dave, Maria, Sean, Jenny, Kim, Mike, Randy, Vanessa, Kathy, George, Rick, Sylvia, Randa, Ronnie, Caroline, Bridget, Heather, Jennifer, Deanie, Stephanie, Barbara, Lisa, Sue, Sam, and so many more of you who have encouraged me on this journey.

Not only have people played major roles in my life, but I also wouldn't be where I am without the unconditional love, caring and majestic strength of the special animals I have been blessed to know. Kitty, Captain, Sammy, Butch, Chanel, Wally, Nicholas, Charlie, Randy, Buffet, George, Fat Pat - you have all showed me love, given me strength to move forward when I didn't know if I could, cuddled me while I cried/fell/and got back up again. I think of you every day and all the wisdom you've shared with me. Pete, Oliver, Ms. Jackson and Mik have taken over for you and are guiding me every day to live fully in the adventure we call life.

I continue to receive confirmations that I'm on my mission to reflect the love, beauty, courage, strength, and leaps that each of you have inside you. What you see in me is what is in you. The love and truth in me sees the love and truth in you. Namaste.

Thank you all!

Sending you love and happy adventures!

Camden

Things can fall apart, or threaten to, for many reasons, and then there's got to be a leap of faith. Ultimately, when you're at the edge, you have to go forward or backward; if you go forward, you have to jump together.

Yo-Yo Ma

A Note from Camden

This is a work of stories of my life

from my remembering and perspective. One thing I've learned in my life is that we can all be sitting in a room together, eating the same meal, having the same conversation, and each of us will walk away with a different story from our time together.

Does that mean that someone is right and someone is wrong? I don't believe so. I believe that from our experiences, we take in through our mind and heart and filter what we need from those experiences, to become the person we are meant to be in our lives. It's not always easy or at a conscious level. When we become conscious of it, we can check in with our belief and ask if this belief is a lie or true for us. The answers are always inside.

We are all on a spiritual adventure. This is the story of mine that took from me from dark to light; from living in reckless extremes and suicide attempts to a life full of love, purpose, prosperity, and service of others. It will take you on a journey of letting go, standing in truth, and connect you to your own evolution and metamorphosis.

Together we stand strong, true, and connected and together we can transform our lives while transforming the world.

Since this is a true story, names and other identifying details of some characters have been changed to protect individual privacy and anonymity.

Rituals

Find a place inside where there's joy and the joy will burn out the pain.

Joseph Campbell

I heard voices sometimes. They were inside my head. They used to tell me to hurry up, hurry up and wash your hands, hurry up and brush your teeth, hurry up and get ready for bed, hurry up and make your bed. If you were a good girl, you would be doing this better. They were always talking and talking, faster and faster and faster. I tried to breathe but it was like the sound of the voices drowned out the fact that I was even breathing.

I panicked and froze.

Voices.

If they were talking to me at night I did bicycle kicks lying in my bed. This also helped me stop the growing pains that hurt so badly in my legs and knees at night. The other thing that helped was saying the rosary.

I started at St. Mary's School in first grade. It was 1972 and my first grade teacher was Sister Ellen. We weren't

Catholic but it was close to our house and a good private school. I loved school. I loved getting ready in the morning and having somewhere to go. I loved to learn. I loved to see my friends. I didn't want to stay home. I didn't want to miss a day of school.

I had my paint bag, new shoes, new pencils, notebooks and I was so ready and at the same time so nervous to meet new kids. I did know some of the kids as we had grown up together and our parents knew each other so it wasn't totally weird to me.

We had uniforms which made it easy for me to get ready in the morning. The tough part was my curly hair. Mom said I didn't have time to wash it or take a bath in the morning so I took my bath at night and this didn't work at all for my hair. It would stick out in so many directions it was embarrassing. Sometimes I would try to wet it in the sink but it just didn't work so I let it be. That's what curly hair wants anyway. It has its own direction and its own way. Not great for school pictures but it is cute now, right?

Right?

Ah, to be six and go to this new place was exciting. I had never really gone to church before let alone been around nuns before. I discovered that I loved nuns. Sister Ellen was the best teacher and she played guitar and sang songs and first grade was so much fun.

We lived in Rome, Georgia. Growing up in the South in the 1970s meant that even though segregation was over, there were black areas of town and white areas of town. St. Mary's was a private school and we only had three black people in all the grades combined 1st through 8th.

Rodney Washington was in first grade with us and he was one of the funniest kids I'd ever met. Sister Ellen would play the guitar and Rodney would stand up in front of the class and sing "The Candy Man Can". I thought he was so brave.

I wasn't brave – the voices told me that.

The voices told me many things – all of them true.

Some of the voices would say "do it" and when I did the

voices said "why did you do that?"

Confusion.

Judgement.

I was walking a tightrope and never quite got it right. It was all mixed up inside me but it was just me so I started to beat myself up. I was doing my best to stay in the middle and ride the centerline. I didn't feel good about myself. I was so out of place I felt like my body belonged to someone else.

I was curious about God. Did I believe? Was I allowed to believe if I wasn't Catholic?

I loved the nuns at school. I loved the mass at school and I knew it all by heart and would silently mouth all the words during the service every Wednesday when the school cafeteria turned into a church. There was something about the rituals which seemed to hold me in a safe space. I was moving and occupied and the voices were mostly quiet except when it was time for communion.

I couldn't take communion. At communion time, each class lined up in front of the priest ready to eat the body of Christ. I didn't really understand how that was the body of Christ but I did understand that I was left out.

I would sit alone waiting for the class to file back one at a time into the metal folding chairs. I was different and left out.

I was curious about confession. I worried that if I didn't go and confess my sins I would go to Hell. Hell didn't sound like a fun place. It was dark and there were bad people there who didn't believe in God. God would punish me if I didn't tell my sins in confession.

I couldn't go to confession and I couldn't take communion. I was different. Not Catholic. I thought about this a lot.

To help us understand that all people are different and what prejudice felt like, we did an interesting exercise all morning until after lunch one day. Sister Ellen split us into groups according to our eye color. I had hazel eyes and we had a fairly big group compared to the size of the other groups. I was excited to see some of my friends in my group and to know that I wouldn't be alone. I did have a really good friend, Eleanor, in a very small group. She had brown eyes. Being in class wasn't so bad because we were in our seats listening and focusing on our studies. Where it got really uncomfortable was at recess and lunch.

We were told not to play with anyone or talk to anyone outside of our group. I had a few friends to play with so I was okay but I did watch my friend Eleanor and a couple of other kids in other eye color groups. Eleanor was crying on the steps and not playing at all. I felt so sad for her and I knew I couldn't go talk to her.

I went to the bathroom and had to go sit alone and take some deep breaths. I didn't want to do to the exercise anymore. It was too hard and even though I had a cool group to play with it didn't feel right leaving out the other kids and ignoring them.

We came in after playing at lunch and had a talk about what we had noticed and what we had learned. We talked about eye color, skin color, all of our differences, and about how we were all different but inside we're all the same. It's only fear that keeps us from being friends and accepting each other as we are.

The wheels started turning in my head and this exercise, this teaching from Sister Ellen had sparked my heart in new ways that would forever affect my life and come back to visit me in just a few years in a moment of complete evil and a moment of complete judgment and fear.

Don't Tell

Until we have seen someone's darkness we don't really know who they are. Until we have forgiven someone's darkness, we don't really know what love is.

Marianne Williamson

It was 1988. I was coming down from a two day cocaine, ecstasy and drinking binge. It was during winter finals at school and I had a final in my constitutional law class that morning. Our teacher challenged us with enthralling spur of the moment questions in class where he randomly asked us to stand and answer thoroughly. I liked him and appreciated his attention and brilliance.

I had an A in the class and he had written a recommendation to law school for me.

I knew I had the final and I went out anyway. I bargained that it was just one night, then it turned into another hour, then another night, then crash. Once I got started, it was hard to stop.

I did my best to pull it together, shower, and get ready. My stomach was acidy and needed food after not eating for two days. I smelled like stale cocaine and had the leftover sticky dry feeling on my gums from the ecstasy. I really hadn't been eating much in the last few months as I had been binging on and off the party circuit. I had a new boyfriend, and between him and his friends, my drug supply was plentiful. I got out of the shower, dressed and realized my lips were swollen, bloody, and cut from chewing them. I looked like I had been hit in the face.

I had to go take the final.

I went to school, walked in the classroom late, the exam had already started. I snuck into my seat. My teacher stared at me with a knowing look. I couldn't hide from him. He knew. I couldn't focus and the words were darting all over the page. I walked to the desk, handed in my exam and walked out.

I had hit a low. I couldn't go back to the sorority house where I was living. It was too much. I called my old boyfriend, Kolton, who was living in Baton Rouge at the dorms at LSU, and asked to see him.

I was alone and didn't know where to go.

He would accept me.

He would comfort me.

He would make it alright.

I tried to do it myself and I failed.

He said I could come over to his room. I drove to his place. I knocked on the door. He let me in his room and locked the door. He had a strange, familiar look in his eye.

The fact that he locked the door made the hair on my neck stand up. Was it that I was so hungover or was it him in this moment?

Something didn't feel right.

I had this same feeling over a year before. We had broken up and gotten back together. I drove to visit him in Monroe to see him and meet his new yellow lab puppy. When I arrived, we hopped in his car and went for a drive. Something was sad about him and very childlike. I felt so bad for him and wanted to make everything alright again.

Take care of him.

Make it all alright again.

The Doobie Brothers were playing in the background and there was an uncomfortable silence. I didn't recognize where we were going and it was far away from town. I asked where we were going. He said to a cool place he wanted to show me and we would let the dog run and play. We pulled up in the middle of nowhere, no one around for miles, no houses, no sounds, not anything.

My hair on the back of my neck stood up. My intuition was telling me something was not right. I thought maybe he was going to kill me or had I just read too many non-fiction books about psychopaths. I knew he had a gun in the glove compartment but he said it wasn't loaded.

He asked me to get out of the car and he called the dog out too. He commented on how I had lost weight and that I looked good. I did feel a little more confident and tried to look nice for him. I had on funky black patent leather lace up shoes and a loose acid washed pink and black striped mock shirt with my "skinny" jeans that I hadn't been able to wear for a while because I was fatter. I also had a new stylish haircut and was feeling pretty good about myself that day.

The voices were approving too.

I felt his compliment and attention melt me and give me hope again that we might work. We might stay together and everything would be fixed. He had changed or so I thought.

Then he started to grab the puppy by the neck as he asked me, "How many guys have you slept with since we've been broken up?"

The puppy yelped and I moved toward him, to free the puppy, but he moved away. Something wasn't right. I could feel it. He might hurt me. I had a feeling that he brought me here to kill me. I had to get out of here. I had to persuade him that I dated only one guy and that it was just a rebound and meant nothing.

I had to downplay everything.

I had to get out of there.

I started to cry because I was afraid but also because I

needed him to snap out of his anger and feel something for me again. I knew we could make it right if we could get out of there and he could get help. I had to make it better.

Here was that feeling again, over a year later. He was going to hurt me and I was too weak, too hungover, and too broken to figure a way out.

His dorm room was small. He pulled me over to the bed, laid on top of me, held me down, pulled my pants down just enough to force himself inside me. I froze, tears streaming down my face. My voice could only talk in a whisper – or was I really even talking at all?

"Stop, you're hurting me. This is not what I came for."

It was as if he was marking me as his territory again.

Voices in my head, "Why did I go to his room?"

He finished and it was over.

I was frightened of this look in his eye I had seen before but this time it was more intensified. Anger, confusion, distant. I was afraid he was going to kill me. I had those thoughts before but dismissed them and forgot. They were back now and I had to trust my intuition.

I remembered just six months earlier, he stormed the sorority house, paranoid on something and ran up and down every hall and in every room looking for me. Our house mother called security and he left before they arrived. I was not in the house that night but was told he was crazed and unreasonable.

Voices in my head, hissing at me.

I had to find a way out of this room. I lied and told him I needed to call Dad, that I needed to go home and get help. I needed to go to rehab. He picked up the phone and asked for Dad's number. He would dial it for me. He told Dad I was there and needed to talk to him. I felt him monitoring me. I told Dad I needed help and I needed him to come get me. The whole time I was watching Kolton, evaluating him.

Dad and I didn't talk long and he said would be on the next plane from Atlanta to Baton Rouge. Dad called back and told me when he would arrive. Relief mixed with more fear. I could get away from Kolton but I had to face my father.

I told Kolton I needed to go shower and pack. He unlocked the door and let me go. I showered him off of me and watched what had happened flow down the drain. I didn't tell anyone.

Dad arrived, he asked me no questions. He looked at me, saw that I had lost about 20 pounds, dark circles under my eyes, and bloody swollen bitten lips. He hugged me and led me to the gate to board the plane to Georgia. Once we were on the plane, I laid my head on his lap, and went to sleep.

We landed in Atlanta and drove the hour home to Rome, where Mom hugged me and asked if I was okay. Looking back, I think she was shocked at my appearance. I was. I didn't recognize the person looking back at me from the mirror – especially from the mirror in my childhood home.

I couldn't look in the mirror long. When I did, I felt vacuumed back, as if I was in a tunnel that was sucking me backwards. I was small and couldn't feel my body.

I didn't want anything to eat and went straight to bed, sleeping until the next afternoon. When Brother got home from school, he came in my room and asked if I was okay. He looked scared for me.

Mom made me something to eat and starting talking about rehab.

"I just need to get my strength back and then we can talk."

In a few days, I sat down with Mom and she asked if I had a problem. That was a loaded question. Yes, I did and I was still mad and too tired to talk about all of them; one of which was her.

I was still angry with her.

I didn't want her help. It always had strings attached to it.

To get her off my back, I told her I didn't have a problem. I didn't need rehab. I needed rest. I called the school and was granted a medical leave for three weeks. I rested. I was ready to get back to school to my friends and classes.

I flew back to Baton Rouge and was ready to be at LSU again. I got right back in the swing. This time not as hard as before. I told myself I could party a little and my roommate said she would be there to pick me up anytime I called and we would help each other stay focused in these last few months of school.

I still had my secret and told no one.

I'm Big Now

A mother always has to think twice, once for herself and once for her child.

Sophia Loren

I learned so much in Sister Ellen's class and couldn't wait to go back to school after the summer. Ms. Maslanka was my second grade teacher and she was so wonderful to us. At the end of the day, she asked us to sit in our desks, put our heads down, and close our eyes. She would tap whoever was good that day with the magic wand. When we lifted our heads and opened our eyes, those of us tapped would get a rubber cigar known as a twizzler. I didn't get one every day. Not everyone did.

The voices were still talking to me but I could muffle them with my bicycle kicks or saying the rosary at night. Thank God I ordered that rosary in first grade. I went to mass every week at school. I had memorized all the words not just the ones we were supposed to say but I had memorized Father Rabbit's words, the altar boys', and the ones we were supposed to know, plus all the songs. The rituals in my head seemed to help keep me grounded and the voices didn't come in as much.

Everyone in my second grade class was Catholic, except for me and one other person. I was still excluded. I just wanted to be a part of something. To belong.

I thought that was what "normal people" did. They went to church and then had a big lunch together at the country club or their mom made a big Sunday lunch. I often went to church with one of my best friends, Mary Alice, and then her mom made a big lunch. There was something nurturing and calming about hanging out with my friend's family. I felt "normal".

Yes, I had a family but there was something different. I knew what one big thing was and I wanted to keep it a secret for as long as I could. Why couldn't we just be like everyone else?

So those voices - I could get them to stop or at least slow down sometime. They filled so much space that I felt suffocated. Playing in the woods and building forts with my friends calmed the voices at times. Most times I just pushed them down the best I could and lived with the voices muffled in my head.

Second grade was when things at home began to change for me with Mom. It was like something clicked inside and I was starting to figure out a pattern. I liked to try to figure things out in my head because it made it easier if I knew what was coming because I could decide what needed to be done.

I knew Mom drank. Dad drank too, but not like Mom. When I was eight years old, I woke up to a different me. Everything changed. Mom, Brother, and I were visiting Mom's parents in Anna Maria Island, Florida, where they lived six months out of the year. I loved visiting them. It was predictable and easy.

Anna Maria Island was a beautiful beach and I was so excited to see my grandparents. There were a lot of old people there and everyone drove very slowly. They ate dinner at four o'clock for the early bird special.

It felt like we were in a time warp.

Other things warped too.

I was very close to my grandparents, especially Nannie, since I was the first grandchild on mom's side of the family. My grandparents called me Cammie. I already loved routine and rituals; the routine of the visit comforted me.

Paw Paw made breakfast, we played Gin Rummy in the sun room, a ride on the boat, bologna sandwich for lunch, some beach time, and after showers, out to dinner for the early bird special and home by 6pm for Lawrence Welk and his bubble machine, then Pat Sajak and Vanna White on Wheel of Fortune. It was a little like a modern day Leave it to Beaver - no problems, no drinking, happy times. Paw Paw made whatever you wanted to eat every morning even if it was pancakes every day. Plus he made milkshakes in the afternoon.

Nannie and I would hang out, and sometimes go out on their boat with homemade sandwiches and do a little fishing. I'll have to say the best part about fishing was casting. I loved mastering throwing the line out and bringing the line in. They also had a cool pet, sort of pet. It was a heron and he would come to the back door every day where Paw Paw would feed him chicken necks he had bought at the grocery. When Paw Paw died years later that bird kept coming to the back door and I hoped that the new owners of the house would take care of him like Paw Paw had loved that bird. Life was simple and fit nicely into my safe space.

I couldn't wait to get to the beach. I was already as tan as a brown berry as Dad's mother, my Neno, used to say. I had olive skin, curly brown hair, hazel eyes which shifted between blue-gray and blue-green. I was curious, a keen observer, and eager to please my parents at this age.

The beach also attracted our cousins and some good friends my parents would hang out with that had kids around our age. It might be a pool party, or we'd go to the lake house, or just someone's house and play most of the day and into the night while our moms got dinner ready, shelling peas, or stringing beans and having some wine. The Dads would watch football, go play golf, waterski, or play with us in the water.

It wasn't so bad when we were with other people because it just seemed that's what adults did to have fun. They would get together talk and drink. They would sometimes fall down, or argue with each other, but no one got hurt so much they would bleed.

Cammie, "the little mom" meant I kept an eye on the other kids and made sure we had something to eat when supper was ready. I made sure we stayed out of the way so we didn't get hurt.

Children are so forgiving and can move on to the next moment fairly quickly at a young age. We trust that our needs are met and our parents are there to love and take care for us. If and when that trust is damaged is when life gets uncertain. Will we get home safe? Will they argue tonight? Will she come in my room and wake me up crying? I better pay attention so I can make sure I'm safe and everybody gets to bed okay.

It was That Day. The day at the beach when everything changed. Nannie and Paw Paw weren't going because it was just too hot for them.

Mom, Brother, and I gathered our towels, made some sandwiches, got the usual beach stuff of umbrella, chairs, and sand toys. It was a hot day with the usual dependable gulf coast breeze. The water was blue as the sky and when you looked out far you couldn't see where one began and the other ended. The sand was soft, white, and great for digging holes and building drip sand castles.

I was excited about the beach, but something was off. Mom was edgy and impatient. I felt a hesitation in my heart. I couldn't pinpoint it exactly but I knew I needed to pay attention. I felt things when I was little and many times they were alert signals to be aware and observe. I was a born observer and so was Brother.

He was more tangible like he knew where everything

was in the house when he was two or three years old. You'd ask where something was and he would go right to it. He was curious.

On the other hand, I was the observer from a different perspective. I would notice people's moods, behaviors, choices, patterns, body language; I could sense what I needed to be in that moment to exist with that person or if I needed to leave them and go somewhere and hide. I felt like I saw things that other people just didn't notice or didn't think were important.

I knew it was all important in the bigger picture of things.

I needed to keep it in my head because it would come in handy later.

Mom was irritated and hurrying to get out of the house. Some friends were in town for the weekend from home and we planned to meet them either at the beach or later for a cookout. The moms could visit and cook and the kids would play together.

We got in the car with all our gear, said our goodbyes to Nannie and Paw Paw, and headed out. Brother was engaged but quiet.

As we drove out of the familiar neighborhood on the water, I glanced at the rock yards with statues in them. Mom said they belonged to tacky Yankees, snowbirds who didn't like to mow the lawn. I had memorized the streets in the neighborhood.

Mom took the left turn toward the drugstore. I thought we were going to buy a raft, or get more sunscreen, or maybe she needed me to go in and get her a carton of Salem Ultralights.

She said she wanted to make a stop. Right next to the drugstore was a liquor store.

She didn't ask me to go in the drugstore.

Instead she said she would be right back. Brother and I waited in the car, the air conditioning on full blast. When she came out, she had a small brown paper bag with a bottle in it.

My heart was in my stomach. I knew.

When she got in the car, I saw the black ridged top of the transparent bottle peeking out from the bag. I knew exactly what it was.

Vodka.

Vodka, because it was easier to hide on her breath.

Vodka, because she could drink it with orange juice and no one would know.

Vodka, because.

I asked her not to drink. She said she would do what she wanted and it would be okay. I knew it wasn't going to be the beach time I wanted it to be. I missed Dad. I wanted to go home. I wanted my grandparents. I also wanted to go to the beach. I would take care of this. I would make sure she didn't drink too much. I would make sure Brother and I were okay.

We carried all our gear to the perfect beach spot, pulled out the sand toys, and set up our towels.

Mom sat in her beach chair. She grabbed the brown bag, holding it down to the side of the chair close to the sand pouring it in her cup like she didn't want anyone to see. I saw. She poured some orange juice in the cup too, put it down beside her chair and lit a cigarette.

It was beach time.

Time to play and keep one eye on Mom and the other on Brother.

After playing in the waves and building a sand castle, we were starving. Swimming always made me hungry. Mom unpacked the picnic. I looked in Mom's cup. Her drink was not as orange as when we first got to the beach. Now it was more clear and watery looking.

Observation and note to self: At home when mom sat on the couch and needlepointed, she would sometimes have this drink, her screwdriver. It would start out orange and over the course of the day it would appear watery and clearer. Her eyes would look a far off and she slurred her words.

One time Nannie and Paw Paw dropped by and Mom

was sitting on the couch doing needlepoint and having her drink. They rang the bell and she opened the cabinet on the table next to the couch and hid her drink in there. Since cataloging this in my brain, I knew something was up with this screwdriver, the watery, orange liquid, or she wouldn't have to hide it.

Here at the beach, she now was drinking the same watery, slightly orange drink as when she was on the couch. When she went to get in the ocean, I looked at the bottle to see how much she had drank. It was half gone.

Mom seemed very relaxed, almost sleepy. She wasn't slurring or falling down. We were still okay.

We were still okay.

About that time, our friends from Rome showed up on the beach and asked us to come to the condo they were renting. The moms would make some dinner and drink some wine and the kids could play.

We packed up at the beach and went straight there. Mom called Nannie and Paw Paw to let them know our plans. At first it was fun. Then it started to get dark. Dark in the sky and dark at the dinner.

Mom hadn't eaten much all day. Her walk was swervy and it was hard for her to stand. Her friend, Deborah, walked her into the back bedroom and closed the door. I was ready to go home. I heard noises in the bedroom and opened the door. Mom was slumped over and Deborah was holding her head while she threw up in the blue plastic garbage can.

Mom looked up and I don't think she knew it was me. Her eyes were vacant and seemed to be going in all different directions. I froze.

The next thing I knew, Paw Paw came to pick us up and drive us home. Did I call him? I think I did but I couldn't remember. They helped him get Mom in the car and Brother and I climbed in the back. No car seats back then or even seat belts.

I crawled into bed to the sound of Nannie getting mad at Mom.

"Elizabeth, you can't keep doing this. You've got to stop drinking."

My brain catalogued it. Nannie and Paw Paw knew the drinking had been going on for some time. Mom hadn't fooled them like she thought she did. What else did they know? Did they know I knew? Was I supposed to do something? I was "the little mom" and I watched out for myself and for Brother.

When Mom woke up, Nannie and Paw Paw had a talk with her about her drinking. I listened by the door but they talked softly so didn't hear much. But I knew she was in trouble and it couldn't be good. She had crossed a line.

I felt bad for her and wanted everyone to be happy.

I was mad at her.

I was scared.

I didn't feel safe and I didn't know when it would happen again but I would be on guard.

If I had just been a good girl, I could have fixed it so she didn't drink.

I was a failure.

When I got older, the voices were still there but they were different. They seemed to be my friend but they weren't very nice to me. They said mean things. They said:

It's your fault.

If you were just a better little girl, your mom wouldn't drink.

You're ugly and no one will like you if they know.

First Kiss

Only those who risk going too far can possibly find out how far they can go.

T.S. Eliot

I sucked my thumb until 5th grade.

It was my security blanket, even though I still had an actual blanket. When my parents would fight at night, or Mom would drink, I could suck my thumb and fall asleep more easily and block out the noise and the voices a little more. Once I started having sleepovers with friends I had to stop sucking my thumb plus I noticed that my teeth were sticking straight out and I didn't want to make it worse. I still had my blanket that I could hold and I could say my rosary at night, more than once, if I needed it.

The voices encouraged me to hide. Shhhh, don't be seen. Watch. Observe.

That's something I felt I was really good at: observing and creating a story that was really a lie but sounded like it could be true. I was a manipulator. For a long time, I asked myself, *was I born this way? Is this a useful skill?*

Yes, at the time it was useful because it kept me from getting in trouble and it certainly kept peace in the family and I really needed peace. I was the family peacemaker and fixer. I was also a perfectionist and an approval seeker and people pleaser.

I was so happy to be in high school and a little nervous too. Harder classes, older guys to meet, dorm students from all over the world offering more excitement, parties, football games, and soon to be driving.

It was my first party that fall. A few of us spent the night with our friend, Julie, and we were going to Richard Marcus' party. We got a ride with Julie's brother.

At the party, everyone was just hanging out, talking, music playing in the background, and there was drinking.

It wasn't new to me.

Drinking.

Drinking wasn't new.

I had taken some from my parents' liquor cabinet before without them knowing. They never noticed it was gone, so it was easy. So easy.

I started talking to people at the party. Someone offered me a beer. I took it and drank it. I had another a little slower this time.

I saw my crush from 8th grade. We were in the same class, but he was a year older; he'd been held back a year, to play sports, I think.

We took a walk and ended up sitting on a hay bale in the side yard, away from the party. He put his arm around me and started kissing me.

I was so nervous and could not believe this was happening. Thank you God for this moment. I knew things were going to be better.

He kept kissing me and around my lips was getting wet with our spit.

My first real kiss.

Then I felt his hand move up my shirt and into my bra, brushing my right boob. Shit. What do I do? This feels odd, and not right, and yet it felt good.

I didn't plan this.

I'm okay.

I can do this.

I flinched backward when his hand touched my boob so that my stomach and boobs became concave. I didn't want to appear inexperienced, so I didn't say anything and he must have thought I was pretty or he wouldn't do this.

He must have thought I was pretty or he wouldn't do this.

I heard someone call my name a few times. It was Julie. She was looking for me. We had to get home for curfew. He and I planned to come out one at a time so no one knew we were together. I went first then he would come a few minutes later. Julie seemed mad and worried that I had disappeared; then I realized she was just worried about curfew.

I was glad to be going home too. I was a little dizzy from the beer and the kiss and all with my crush. It was a big night. I felt older somehow.

High school was here and so was I.

Summer, Horses, Freedom

Do not go where the path may lead, go instead where there is no path and leave a trail.

Ralph Waldo Emerson

I watched the Wizard of Oz when I
was four years old. I was with my parents at our weekend cabin at Lake Weiss and it was Easter. The movie came on TV every year at that time. So many people waiting for Easter to watch this movie and we were all watching it together. The colors in the movie were so bright and life-like to me.

I loved Toto and when Miss Gulch took Toto away from Dorothy I was so sad and I was scared of her. But what really made me cry was when Dorothy threw water on the wicked witch. I can still hear her voice "I'm melting, I'm melting." I was crying and very upset about this. How sad that she never got a chance to be accepted and loved for whom she was. I felt so sad for her.

My parents said she was a bad witch so it was okay that she was dead. I disagreed.

Didn't everyone deserve to be happy?

Didn't everyone deserve to be loved? Didn't everyone deserve to be accepted?

The theme that went through my thoughts each Easter I watched the Wizard of Oz was that Dorothy was swept away in the tornado and on her adventures on the yellow brick road; she had experiences and met people on her path that helped her put the puzzle pieces of herself together. They helped her remember what home was and where it was. That was something I wanted to know.

I was ready to leave when I was eight. I was going to one day move to New York City. It was a place that I had seen on TV, that I knew was far away and that was very sophisticated. I was going. At eight I would settle for two weeks away at Camp Juliette Lowe where I spent some of the best summers of my life.

Summers meant freedom.

Summer for me was a time to get away from the unpredictable happenings at home. I got to be a kid for real. I didn't have to think about if Mom was drunk when I walked in the door with a friend to come play. I slept well at night and didn't hear my parents fighting.

At camp we woke up early and took cold showers and ran to raise the morning flag and get ready for breakfast before a day of activities. We even used an outhouse and didn't have a toilet but this was part of the beauty of camp. Camp was simple.

You came, had a blast, made friends, and did cool activities all day like sailing, knot tying, archery and diving. We had special activities too. We would have campfire sing-a-longs at night. We went on overnight campouts and slept under the stars.

One summer I was a bit of a celebrity because I had a bat living above my bed in the tent. He was there the entire four weeks and never dropped on me or left. He became my friend and it was pretty cool to have him there.

Camp Juliette Lowe was a Girl Scout camp on Lookout Mountain which is shared by three states: Alabama,

Georgia and Tennessee. We were in the Alabama portion and I loved the drive from Rome through Summerville, Georgia to get there.

My friend Rema and I went together and each year we shared a tent with two other girls. The tents were on platforms with a large forest green canvas over the top so it was sort of camouflaged in the canopy of trees which leaves ranged in color from chartreuse to jade green. It was our very own tent except for bugs sometimes and the occasional critter that we didn't see but could hear scurry past making swishing noises outside the brown planks that made up the floor of our tent.

There were other tents each with four girls too. There were four wire beds, which were really sturdier cots. We each had a shelf to put our things on and a steamer trunk for our clothes fit neatly under our cots.

On nice, sunny days, which were most days, we rolled the sides of the tents up neatly and tied them to stay. That was one of my favorite parts. There were no walls. The lush green forest branches and leaves were our walls.

I felt at home since we'd been making forts in the woods near our homes in Rome after school almost every day.

After lunch in the cafeteria and the daily mail call, we came back to our cots to rest before our afternoon activities. The wind would usually pick up in the afternoon. The breeze through the branches billowing through our tent was calming and cooling. It dried the sweat that caught on my body after running back from mail call with my daily mail and ice cream shaped like Mickey Mouse. His ears were chocolate, his face was vanilla with chocolate eyes. I had one every day after lunch.

At the beginning of each session, we chose the activities we wanted to take for the two week session. It was fun to coordinate with friends and meet new friends too. We had so many to choose from: Arts & Crafts, Archery, Lashing, Knot Tying, Diving, Tennis, Sailing, Canoeing - those were some of my regulars.

Everyone at camp got to take horseback riding. While I

liked it because I liked the horses, there was a part of me that dreaded it too.

I was scared of horses.

I hadn't been around horses and they were so big.

I just didn't know what to do around them.

I felt out of control.

I wasn't sure of myself.

I didn't take lessons at home. I did know of a horse in a field in the woods near our house. He was white. He was alone. One time he got out and took off running down the trail toward the road. Luckily, the owners caught him and put him back. I think he was lonely and wanted some attention. I was afraid he would run over me.

At camp, we rode different horses in each lesson. It was hard because I felt just when I was getting to know one horse they switched it out on me. I was shy and didn't want to ask questions when I was in our group lesson. I did my best to listen to the instructor and follow directions. I could feel I was tense when I was on the horse. I didn't want to fall off. There were some girls who were really graceful and rode so well. That was not me but I did do my best even being afraid. I loved animals and I felt like there was something there for me.

During every session, we got to go on a trail ride into the woods. On the trail, it was important to stay in the middle of the trail, single file, one horse length from the horse in front of me and behind me.

Once my horse drifted to the right to try to munch a green leaf branch. The horses loved trying to sneak a bite when they thought you weren't paying attention. He got me this time. He got the bite and my leg rubbed hard against a tree. It hurt. I didn't cry though. I didn't want to get off and have to go to the infirmary. I got him back to the middle of the trail and let it go. We kept riding.

Even though I was scared, I also felt at ease inside. It didn't make sense to me but it sort of did, or I wouldn't have kept riding.

Every summer I would ride at camp. Every time I would

go back I would have that feeling of excitement and fear combined.

It was like the horses knew what I needed.

I wish I knew what I needed.

For the first two weeks of August every summer, our family rented a cottage at Sea Island, Georgia. Dad would bring home an envelope from the office and show us the brochure with photos of the cottage where we were going to stay. Brother and I each had our own room, and we got to invite a friend too.

I invited Rema every year. At the cottage, we went to the stables to pet the horses. I loved petting the horses. And the beach trail ride. To go on the ride, you had to be able to trot in the ring and control your horse.

I was called to the mounting block to get on my horse. I climbed on and was led into the riding ring, which was right next to Frederica Road. It was the only road on the island that went from one end to the other, so it could get packed and people could see us ride when they were stopped at the stop light waiting to go.

They asked me to trot my horse.

I kicked and he started to trot. At camp, I had learned to use my reins and felt pretty comfortable in the ring. I passed and was told I could go on the beach trail ride.

Rema went to the mounting block. I could see her head when I glanced over. I recognized her because she had gotten a new "Dorothy Hamill" haircut. Her haircut had started to expand since we arrived in the humid, hot beach air. We had teased her that it was growing. I could relate. My hair was curly too but not as curly as Rema's. Her mom was from Egypt and she had curlier hair than I did. She got on her horse and was led to the ring. They asked her to trot.

I was on the other side of the ring and looked over to see her hair bobbing up and down so fast and Rema sliding to one side of the saddle with her reins in the air trying to slow her horse down.

Do I laugh? Rema was my friend but her hair was funny, like a cartoon.

Soon, they lined us up to cross Frederica Road into the woods that led to the marsh and then to the beach.

Rema was not in line. She didn't make the trail ride. She stayed in the ring for a short lesson while I took to the trail. I felt so bad for her and I missed her. I also had to snap out of that because I needed to pay attention. There was a lot to take care of on the trail. I needed to stay a horse length from the horses both in front of me and behind me. I needed to watch for animals jumping out that might make my horse spook.

Pay attention.

Stay in line.

Don't think about Rema.

Observe.

Once on the beach when we cantered, I needed to make sure my horse didn't go too fast. Again, I was nervous but having fun. I think this is what they call the thrill of the adventure. I loved cantering on the beach, feeling the horse's hooves landing in the sand, and hearing the waves crash next to us.

It also scared me. I didn't want to go too fast.

I still needed to be in control.

I needed to be in control.

I was bummed when we got back and it was over and I was also relieved that I was safe. I had done it. Another summer of riding. Until next summer. I would hold on to the adventure but I knew the fear would rise again. I wouldn't ride again until Summer Camp next year.

Knowing Me

A daughter needs a Mom who will provide her with memories that last forever.

Gregory Lang

My parents and Nannie and Paw Paw

all had locks on their liquor cabinets.

Locks I later learned how to pick.

If Mom had been drinking during the day it was vodka and orange juice, then in the afternoon she would switch to box wine or Gallo in the big green bottle. She didn't drink everyday at first. It was usually every other day so I was able to keep track of it pretty well. I also knew if she felt bad the next day because she would want me to stay home from school with her.

I did when I was young, but then I figured out it wasn't fun. But I didn't want her to feel bad so I stayed. She would pull me into bed with her and hold me and sometimes she would cry. The room was dark and very cold. She liked to keep the house really cold and the windows would fog up in the summer. I would freeze in our house and had a thick down quilt to stay warm at night.

The pattern continued with Mom drinking, Dad working and playing golf and going out of town, and me doing my best to hide the fact that we were not a perfect family. I didn't want to stay home with Mom anymore on those days that she felt bad. I made sure I was up early, dressed, and had eaten breakfast so that Dad could drop me at school which was not too far from our house.

A few times she caught me and made me stay home and I would softly cry as she held on tight to me. It didn't like being with her like this. She was sad and I just wanted to go to school where I was happy and I could be with my friends.

I loved school.

St. Mary's inspired me to learn and grow in my studies and I was curious and I wanted to please.

I also wanted to get good grades so my parents would be happy with me.

Please be happy with me.

At night sometimes, she would drink after dinner. I had gone to bed and then I would wake up and hear sounds in the kitchen. I would hear Mom talking and slurring her words so I would sneak to see what was going on. She would have the phone book, a glass of wine, and her cigarettes at the round kitchen table. She was just calling people she knew to talk.

I would ask her to please go to bed that she was being loud and we needed to get some sleep. She would call me over to her and hug me and cry and tell me how much she loved me. I couldn't stand it. I was sad for her. I felt smothered and I just wanted to get away. That's when I decided when I got older I was going to move far away. I was going to be a business woman, work, and make my own money and wear great clothes. Nobody was going to tell me what to do. I was going to take care of myself.

I was not sure if I wanted to have children.

I began to recognize patterns in her days and nights. I could maneuver and manipulate around these patterns and land safely at school, home, and in bed at night.

I also made sure Brother was all set when we were little too. I was three and a half years older. I was "the little mom" so I had to take care of him.

Brother was a little booger and so quiet too. Mom often didn't know where he was in the house. He was still that curious little rascal and knew where everything was. When he was very little and we lived in our first house as a family in Horseleg Estates, as a baby Brother would crawl out of his room into the kitchen and pull everything out of the cabinets. There was not really any childproofing at that time.

Not like when I had my girls and childproofed everything from the wall sockets, to securing the dressers to the wall, to cabinet closures, and more. With no childproofing, my parents decided to childproof on their own since Brother could get out of his crib while they were sleeping. They bought a huge metal grate that fit on top of his crib. When they would put him to bed, they put the grate on top thinking he would be safe.

I taught him how to push with his head flat to the metal grate and throw the grate off the crib. Then it was easy for him to get out. They were onto him so then they put a lock on the grate and there was a key they kept in their bedroom. I would sometimes get the key, unlock it, and he was free.

He was free.

Free.

I had lost so much weight and my stomach hurt all the time. While I was home, I was sullen, drawn to my bed to sleep, always nervous about what others were thinking of me and ready to get back to LSU.

I talked to my friends at school letting them know how I was doing and keeping up with what was happening while I was away. I missed them. I missed the normalcy of classes and the routine at school.

I didn't tell them what had happened with Kolton.

I felt under a microscope with Mom and I needed to get my strength back and go back to school where I had some freedom and control. I told my parents I didn't need rehab. I knew I wasn't going to rehab because my past experiences with it had not been helpful. I had visited boyfriends there, plus Mom, and our family therapy experience, and I knew it was not going to help me. I could figure it out myself.

Dad suggested I see a psychiatrist in town that he thought could talk to me and maybe help me with some of the things I was stressed about. I went to the appointment and we talked. I told Dr. Courier some of the things that were going on with my breakup with Kolton, stress of school, and I told him about some of the drugs.

I didn't tell him everything, only what I thought he needed to know. The information I shared was censored because I couldn't tell him everything.

What would he think of me?

What kind of girl would he think I was?

He might tell my parents and they wouldn't let me go back to school. I wanted to go back to school. I needed to go back to school.

Dr. Courier was kind and a good listener. He recommended an Esophagogastroduodenoscopy, also called an EGD or upper endoscopy. He would put me under, stick a lighted tube or endoscope in my mouth, down my throat into my esophagus, and look at my stomach and duodenum (the first section of the small intestine) to see if there was damage. He'd also be checking if there was something like a peptic ulcer causing my constant stomach pain.

I went in for the procedure, got prepped, and don't remember a thing. After it was over, he said I didn't have any problems, and he didn't see any damage or anything that would cause the stomach pains I had described to him.

There was no ulcer.

He did tell me he was shocked about something. He said I talked the entire time the endoscope was in my mouth.

When I heard that my stomach clenched and I thought

"Shit, what did I say. Did I tell him anything about what happened with Kolton? Did I tell him I had actually done more partying that I had shared with him? Did I tell him anything about my parents? Did I tell him I was bad? What did he think of me?"

My mind was racing and I wasn't present. I wasn't all there. I was back then and at the same time I was thinking of how to fix it if I did tell him that. I was miles in the past and miles in the future in just a moment. The words jumped a little too quickly and eager from my mouth and I asked him "What did I say? Did I say anything you can tell me?"

He smiled and said, "I couldn't understand a word you said because you had the endoscope in your mouth, but you kept talking and talking."

I felt my stomach release its tension to a familiar mild hold. I felt some ease. I also knew this was a warning to me.

Don't ever get out of control.

Ever.

You can never let anyone know these things about you.

It's too risky.

They'll never accept you and you'll never have what you want.

Stay in control.

Stay in control.

Dr. Courier prescribed Xanax for me and recommended I take a pill up to twice a day for anxiety and depression. I went home and slept. The sleep did wonders for me and I started to eat more and taste certain foods again. I hadn't taken the Xanax yet. I didn't want to be out of control around my parents and I wasn't sure how it would make me feel.

What if I got too chatty around them and said some things I would regret? I couldn't take the chance.

Stay in control.

After a couple of weeks of rest, I was feeling ready to go back to school. I had been talking to my friends Bridget, Caroline, and Heather and it was time to get back. It was my senior year and they told me a guy I was seeing was starting to see someone else while I was gone. I was jealous. My stomach started to hurt and was tied in knots. I was angry and getting all worked up about what to do.

I had to get back.

I had to stop him from leaving me.

I had to be in control.

I took a Xanax. I was tranquilized but not tranquil.

That night, we were going to the country club as a family to eat dinner and spend time with Nannie and Paw Paw, who were in town. I had an hour or so to get changed and be ready to go. I liked going to the club to eat. I didn't like running into people we knew too much, especially right now.

How did I explain me being home from school?

A short winter break - that's it.

We had short breaks for Mardi Gras and other things so they would believe me. That's what I will tell them if they ask.

I got dressed in one of my favorite outfits and pair of shoes I bought last summer while I was studying abroad in London. It was a form-fitting skirt of dark brown, soft ribbed t-shirt material. There was a black stripe down the outer hemlines of the skirt. It was slimming and showed off my skinniness in just the right ways since losing some weight.

The top was simple, with buttons down the front and a circular black outline along the scoop collar. It was trendy and very European. Nothing like it in Rome, Georgia.

I liked being different with my style.

I liked being noticed.

I liked being seen.

And then I didn't.

It was a constant hide and seek in my life. I was afraid to be seen for who I really was but I wanted to be seen. I was afraid if anyone knew the real me they wouldn't like me. Did I even know the real me?

Dinner was like a dream. Connie, who was the hostess

that night, greeted us when we arrived at the dining room.

"Hi, Mr. Jones, Mrs. Jones. Hi Camden, Frank, everyone. It's so good to see you tonight." She was black and had worked at the club for many years. She was so nice, had a beautiful smile and incredibly dark luminous skin. She remembered everyone's names and always made us feel welcome and that she was genuinely happy to see us. She took care of everything we needed when we were there.

I had a thought. This was the same country club that asked me and my friends Mike and Steve to leave because Steve was black just back in 1984. Just four years earlier. This was so two faced and wrong. I pushed the thought away. I had already made a scene four years ago about this at the club that day and talked to Dad about it. I was told that's the way it is right now. It's just understood that black people don't come to the club socially.

I stuffed back down the memories and thoughts I was having.

This was not the night or time for bringing up this again. Connie showed us to our table and stepped away momentarily. She came back with my favorite appetizer to munch on while we looked at the menus. Saltine crackers baked with parmesan cheese on top. So simple, so delightful, and my stomach was growling. I had three right away.

We were waiting on Nannie and Paw Paw to arrive. They knew I was home and they knew why. Not all the details, but enough that Nannie was worried. Nannie always worried. She worried if I had enough money. She worried about me and boys. She worried about Mom and if she would drink again. She worried about how Dad treated Mom. She worried about how much Dad worked and played golf.

As she got older, I noticed she didn't seem as happy as when we were younger. She often had a look in her eyes that she was taking care of something somewhere else.

It was good to see them that night as they arrived and sat

down across from me at the table. Paw Paw was quiet, as always. He stuttered when he talked and had talked that way since he was a boy. He would flip a small silver pocket knife smaller than my pinkie finger to get the syllables caught in his mouth to come out and form into words. Sometimes he stuttered more and sometimes less. He had a gray goatee always and gray balding hair. He prided himself on his impeccable southern style sometimes in white slacks with a light weight pink jacket and matching tie and others in a debonair navy blazer and sharp plaid pants.

He had a kind face and always had a silly joke to share that made you laugh with him. He was a breakfast and milkshake master and when I would spend the night with Nannie and Paw Paw whether it was in their apartment in Rome or their house in Anna Maria Island, Florida, he was the best short order breakfast cook and the best at mixing my favorite vanilla milkshakes.

Memories were flooding in and some sadness about how I had disappointed my family. I was a fuck up. I was a black sheep. They didn't even know me. They knew what I let them know about me. I kept them at a distance and let them in only as much as I felt safe.

I was a fuck up.

I was a black sheep.

They didn't even know me.

I was a fuck up.

I was a black sheep.

They didn't even know me.

I started to tear up. Where did I go? Where have I been?

The first Xanax must not be working. I excused myself to the bathroom and took another pill, took a deep breath, a quick wash of hands, and smoothing of my skirt in the full length mirror. All set. Time to go back to dinner.

The conversation was all on the surface. We talked about school. My plans of law school, interning in D.C., and what was I thinking of doing after law school. I shared my excitement to get back to LSU and graduate.

37

I explained I wouldn't be going to graduation. I would get my diploma in the mail. Everyone was fine with that plan. That way I kept all areas of my life and people separate and in control. No one to micromanage me and tell me what to do.

Even though it felt in control, it also made me sad. I wanted to be a normal family where my parents came to Parent's Weekend. Normal families came to graduation and it was fun.

But that wasn't the way it was. If it was a family event, it wasn't fun. It was uncomfortable. We kept so much bottled up inside and what you saw was not what you got. It looked normal on the outside but on the inside it was a holy mess. It's like if you stuff a closet full of so much stuff and you open the door, everything falls out. I was stuffed and continuing to stuff.

What was normal anyway?

Okay, now I felt something.

I think the Xanax was hitting me now.

I started to feel very heavy in my body almost like I was glued to my chair.

The food arrived and before I was hungry and now I felt like a sponge had exploded in my stomach and there was no room for anything. My hands didn't feel like they were on my body when I picked up my fork to push food around on my plate. It felt like these hands belonged to someone else, something mechanical was making them pick up the fork, shove the food to different areas of the plate, creating space so it looked like I was eating.

I took a bite here and there to make it look real.

I couldn't hear well. I was in a tunnel and as people spoke the words were suspended and thick. As I was sitting there, I had a vision that my head fell into my plate and I thought for a moment it was real. It wasn't.

It must be that both Xanax were kicking in now. It was too much and I wasn't going to make it through this without falling asleep. I told Dad I needed to go home and I was tired. Everyone understood and they finished their meal and we went home. I fell asleep in the car on the way home.

This time I wasn't worried if we would crash and die like when I was little. I was crashed and it would be okay if I didn't wake up.

It would be okay if I didn't wake up.

It would be okay.

I somehow made it to my bed and woke up the next morning. Dad came in to see me and asked if I was okay. I told him I think the Xanax was a little strong. He said to call Dr. Courier and ask if there was something lighter than Xanax but still effective that I could take and have when I went back to school. The doctor prescribed Librax and while it helped to relieve my anxiety, it didn't knock me out like Xanax. I still needed to be in control.

I was ready to get back to school to my friends and classes. I flew back and got right back in the swing. My constitutional law teacher made a special arrangement so I could take my exam. I was so thankful because I didn't want to ruin my chances of going to law school when I had worked so hard and other people had written recommendations and encouraged and supported me. He talked to me and was so understanding. I aced my exam. I was so happy to be back. I felt in control. I felt things were looking up.

I felt ready to go out with friends. This time I made a deal to stay more in control. I made a pact with Bridget, Caroline, and Heather and asked them to stop me if I started going too hard. I needed their help. We agreed to help each other. If someone had been drinking too much, just call and we will come get you anytime. We were there for each other. It was our senior year. I had more friends this year. New boyfriends. Kolton was in the past and was no longer controlling me. I felt a freedom I had missed and I could find more of me. I was graduating and it was time to have fun.

Freedom.

Control.

Freedom. Control.

Freedom control.

I told myself I could party a little and keep it under control. I still had my secret about what happened and told no one. I stuffed it deep inside. When I had glimpses or reminders, I would push it back down as far as I could with whatever was handy and numbing at the time. I kept drinking and taking drugs but kept it at a level that I believed was controllable. It never got that out of hand at school again.

I had my Librax which helped with my anxiety and helped come down off a cocaine or ecstasy high too so I could sleep. I shared some with friends who needed the edge off and needed sleep. Those last few months at school were what I had in my mind school was about.

Studying and doing well in school.

Drinking and partying with friends.

Hanging out and dating guys that were fun, normal and great to be around.

They didn't hit me, tell me I was stupid, or abuse me in any way. It was easy, fun, casual sex until I tried to make it more than it was. I wasn't looking for more. I wasn't looking for anyone to save me. I just wanted to live in the moment.

Wasn't life supposed to be easier and not so hard all the time?

That was it and it was almost over. I was finally getting to a place in college where I felt more confidence and I wasn't hiding myself as much. A part of me was coming back that I thought I had lost. Something was changing. I was starting to accept myself more than I had before even in the midst of all the secrets. I could pretend for periods of time that they didn't exist and then I felt what I imagined normal to feel like. I wondered, *Does this come with age or from wisdom gained from life experience or both?* I was willing to keep moving with my life in this moment.

Inside the Beltway

Opportunities to find deeper powers within ourselves come when life seems most challenging.

Joseph Campbell

In 1988, I graduated from LSU and was accepted into law school at a small school in Mississippi. Before law school, I planned to live in Washington D.C. for the Summer and work as an intern for Congressman Buddy Darden from Georgia. It was a non-paying internship and I thought it would be helpful in understanding the law from this perspective. I trusted the feeling and psyched myself up for the move.

I was nervous and excited.

This was my time to firmly put it all behind me. To become the new woman – not Cammie, not "the little mom", not her.

I was registered to live in the dorms at Georgetown University while working on Capitol Hill. I arrived and walked into my dorm room. It was filthy, cigarette butts on the floor, trash in my room, a thin mattress on the bed, and outside my window rap music so loud I could barely hear myself think.

It was too much. I didn't know anyone and I freaked. This was not my new start.

I called Dad and asked if I could check into a hotel. I checked into the Hyatt in Rosslyn, Virginia just over the bridge from D.C. It was next to the metro so it would be easy to get to work every day. My plan was to stay with some friends I knew once they got back from out of town. I lived at the Hyatt for two weeks, a little longer than I thought, then moved in with my friends in their apartment in Alexandria.

We had so much fun together, three girls out of college, working, socializing, and making our way in the world.

I felt I had turned a corner.

My parents were pleased with me.

I was in control.

It was going so well that after my internship ended, I decided to defer law school for a year and get a job on the Hill. I interviewed with several different people on Capitol Hill, and I got a job with a congressman from Stockton, California; Norman Shumway. I started as the receptionist, answering the phones, scheduling White House tours, FBI tours, and other tours for constituents. I was so proud of myself and was excited to be making money and felt I was making a difference.

My parents were not very thrilled that I had deferred law school and they used to joke with me and say, "Well at least when we pay our taxes we can think that we're paying your salary."

In Congressman Shumway's office, I felt a patriotic sense as we worked with passion and dedication to our congressman and to the country to do our best and lead with integrity. It felt powerful and meaningful. During the day I was all work. I arrived on time, was responsible to doing my best. Being the born observer that I was, I took on the challenge to notice everything around me to grow but to also fit in to this new place.

I still wasn't completely comfortable with being my own me and I was still discovering what and who that was. Even though I made this big move I knew there were things I would need to do to fit in and be good.

There were parts of me that wanted to explore and be more. Sometimes from the people pleaser me and wanting approval from my parents that I was finally a good girl and sometimes from the sacred place inside me that knew there was something meant for just me but if I followed that for just me, was that being selfish. I knew selfish was not being a good girl and I was starting to be a good girl. I couldn't wreck everything now.

Don't wreck it.

Don't wreck it.

At times, this fight inside me was impossible to ignore. Being the good girl was what I knew would make my parents happy, or what I believed would make them happy. This mold of the good girl was stifling. It wasn't that I wanted to be bad. It's just I had this image of good and bad and I didn't feel like I fit in either place but somehow always seem to slip between the two. There was no middle road or flow. Couldn't there be gray?

Couldn't there be colors in the gray?

Why did it have to be so divided and why couldn't I just color outside the lines and be okay with it?

My take on Washington, D.C., was that it was very conservative, navy and black business suits, law, order, and power. I wasn't conservative but it was appealing. I wanted to be acceptable and learn more about how it all worked. I was intrigued at the layout of this new land inside the Capital Beltway.

I met so many new people through friends from school and the SEC party they held every year in the Fall. All the SEC schools got together in a hotel ballroom for a party to kick off football season. Each school had its own area of the ballroom and had drinks, some food, cups with logos, school colors - the whole nine yards. We felt a kinship over a common interest of LSU and football. We knew some friends and met some new friends too.

This is where I met Eric.

He was tall, dark, and handsome and worked as a legislative aide to Senator Johnston from Louisiana. He was attentive, kind, and we started seeing each other. I could feel that he cared about me and it made me nervous. When he started to share anything deep or how he felt about me and us, I deflected the conversation to something else.

I was intimate with him but I avoided intimacy. I couldn't let him or anyone get too close. I didn't trust them. I didn't trust that what they said was true or they would be there for me so I created a wall around me. I didn't trust myself. If I tried to keep things in my control, I felt safer. I felt like I had the reins and could escape when I needed to if I felt threatened or smothered.

One night he cooked me dinner at his house. We had beautiful wine, delicious dinner, fun flirty exchanges. Then he picked me up in his arms, carried me to the backyard where he laid out a blanket under a tree. He carefully placed me down on the blanket and loved me softly and tenderly. I felt myself let go of a thread of control but felt unsure and exposed.

Could I be me?

Was it enough?

Who was I?

I had never had a man treat me so nicely and almost every bone in my body said "Don't trust it, it won't last, take control before it's too late."

Why did I have this feeling? Why did I think he was like all the rest? Would he abandon me? I wanted to return to my old pattern because that's what I knew. I knew how to be when someone used me and didn't really care. I knew how to be abandoned. I knew how to feel the void and temporarily fill it with something to numb the pain.

A few weeks passed and we continued to have fun at parties and he continued to be kind, too kind. I was getting uncomfortable with all the kindness. Then he said something that pushed me over the edge, "Camden, I'm falling in love with you."

That was it. Retreat. Chest pounding, heart racing.

I can't do this.

It's too much.

How did this happen?

Why did this happen?

What did I have to offer and why would he love me?

I fell over the edge. I'm selfish. I'm not beautiful. I'm not smart. I didn't say anything, I looked down and withdrew inside myself. I froze. He asked if it was too soon to talk about love. I didn't want to talk about it so I fell back to what I knew. I took back control, gave him a long kiss, and said I'm tired let's go to bed.

After that night and his declaration of love for me, I retreated. I found his kindness offensive and over the top. I was mean and found everything wrong with him. I could not be that woman who he loved. I wasn't that woman, was I? I needed control and he was just too nice. He wasn't my normal pattern of "bad boy" boyfriends who used and abused me.

The voices came back into my head and I listened to them again. There was no way I was good enough for him. We stopped seeing each other.

In the meantime, my old boyfriend from college, Kolton, had been calling me. He came to visit me. I slept with him. Maybe everything would change. It would be different. He hadn't meant to hurt me.

I was manipulating to make my life what I thought life was supposed to be. After a day of sightseeing, he started to act crazy, and accused me of doing cocaine because he said there was white powder on the dash of my car. This was insane. He was insane.

In that moment, I woke up. I saw that he was delusional. I asked him to leave and he flew out the next day. I told him I didn't want to see him anymore. He was mad but I knew something wasn't right with him.

Three days later I got a call from his psychiatrist who told me that I ruined his life and that I shouldn't have treated him that way. It was a strange conversation and something wasn't quite right. He wasn't acting like a psychiatrist should act with a patient. He was acting like a hurt lover, which I learned they were after a phone call with Kolton's brother.

Kolton had had other male partners.

I thought about our dating; I hadn't known but I had known. Something had been wrong. We would visit a friend of his sometimes and when we were all together getting high, I thought they acted strange with each other. I just ignored it and tried to be happy Kolton had a friend. He didn't have many friends and was isolated.

When we were apart at different colleges, he lived with a guy. When I went to visit him, I saw there was only one bedroom and he slept on the couch. When I walked into the apartment I had a strange feeling and I couldn't put my finger on it. Now I knew. I was in denial. I didn't want to see what was clearly in front of me. He was gay or bisexual. The problem I had was that he lied to me.

Kolton had had male partners.

When I found this out, I went through a series of HIV testing over a period of months and had relieving news. I was clear. Why would it take me so long to learn this lesson?

I had no boundaries.

Why didn't I trust my intuition?

Why didn't I see?

He said all the right things and I walked into the unhealthy, repeated, predictable steps I had walked before.

I wasn't worthy of love.

I was ugly.

I was worthless.

Be in control.

Be in control.

Reinvent myself. Be a good person so my parents would be happy with me.

Please be happy with me.

I had a good job. I was wearing preppy Ann Taylor

clothes. I was preppy, and I wasn't punk anymore. I thought my parents would think I was a good person.

Be a good person.

After the HIV tests came back negative, I became involved with a man who worked for Congressman Shumway too. He was so polite, dressed impeccably, good at his job, and I respected his drive for his work and his attention to detail.

There was one problem. He was engaged and was to be married soon. He shared that he was not sure about his marriage and I shared with him that I cared for him. He called off his marriage and our relationship was off to a very rocky start with his friends and ex very unhappy about his decision.

We married a year and a half later in May, 1991. I was twenty-five years old.

Mom planned the whole wedding. I picked out my dress, but I didn't want to ruffle any feathers, so I went with it all, which wasn't like me. Dad and I were waiting in the small room off the foyer of the Presbyterian Church on St. Simons Island, Georgia. My armpits were dripping sweat. I was teary and so emotional and not feeling it in a good way.

Dad was getting ready to walk me down the aisle and he looked at me and he said, "Are you sure you want to do this?"

I walked down the aisle after fanning my armpits with a box top that I found on the floor. The bridal march began to play. Dad took my arm and we begin to walk. I couldn't stop crying. Something didn't feel right but I had to make it right so I did it anyway. I gave myself away again.

My husband was kind many moments, and was very doting and very loving, and then at other moments he was angry. Angry at his mother on the phone. Angry at me but really angry at himself. It was too much to take full time care of a wife and a mother, I thought.

He would call me idiot and stupid. I was very immature in the relationship. He was frustrated with his mother and talked to her every night and this had a negative impact on our life. He loved her and he yelled at her while he talked to her every night. I retreated to talking to Mom everyday. I talked to my mother everyday and she and I nitpicked everything that was wrong with my marriage and life and how it could be better. I made him wrong so I could be right. I was deep in denial of the codependent path I was taking.

I was becoming my mother.

I tried to control everything. I wanted to change him. I wanted to change the way he dressed and the way he looked. I wanted to fight everything.

I got pregnant and had a miscarriage at 10 weeks. I was devastated and felt very alone. We started to fight more and he was verbally abusive. One day I asked myself is this what marriage is? I asked myself what I loved about him. I knew that he would never cheat on me and I felt safe.

Was that love or was it security and was that enough?

Was that a reason to spend the rest of my life with him like this?

We went to counseling, we went to different seminars to work on our marriage but I remembered getting to this point and I just couldn't do it anymore. We woke up on a Saturday morning and were heading to Camden Yards in Baltimore to watch the Orioles play with some of his clients. He asked me, "Are you ready to go the baseball game?"

I said, "I'm not going, I'm leaving."

"What do you mean, where are you going?"

And I said, "I'm leaving you, I'm not going to do this anymore" and I left.

I walked out of the house and called a friend and asked her if I could stay.

Namaste

Yoga is a mirror to look at ourselves from within.

B.K.S. Iyengar

As we walked into the lobby of the

Hotel Wailea to check in for our stay, I smelled yoga. The Nag Champa incense was generously filling the tropical air but not overpowering. After a ten hour plus travel day with Luke and the girls, I was so ready for a yoga practice to relieve the jet lag and soothe my mind into retreat mode.

I had earned the Hawaii holiday with a network marketing company I was working with and to enhance the vacation, we decided to add some days to the beginning of the trip. As we approached the registration desk to check in, I asked, "Is there a yoga retreat happening here right now? Do you know if I could register for a day?"

The beautiful sun-kissed tan woman behind the desk answered, "There is, it's a yoga and raw food retreat. You can go downstairs and meet the two ladies who are in charge of the food. They should be able to help you."

I told Luke while he checked in that I was going to go

49

and check it out and be right back. I walked through the open air lobby down the stairs to a room that was open in the front looking toward the Japanese garden inspired grounds and the ocean. While turning left I saw the two women collaborating food prep against a stunning waterfall and lush plant backdrop as the back wall of the room. Already I was feeling invited and called even.

I asked them if I could join the retreat still, if it was open to hotel guests. They motioned to the other side of the room for me to go and talk to Peter. He was the organizer. I walked over and asked Peter if I could join. He was very nice and said I could come join for $25 a day for the yoga. I was thinking how perfect our trip had started.

Going back to my family, I asked Luke if he would play with the girls while I went to the retreat the next day. He was happy to take them to the beach and we could meet up later. I gave him a long hug, so happy to have arrived, so grateful to know and feel his love, and so ecstatic to enjoy a yoga practice with others to unwind.

I walked to the lovely room with the waterfall and placed my mat down near the center of the other mats already lined up neatly and organically. I walked to fill my water bottle, use the bathroom, and get ready for the class. Before class I always needed to go to the ladies' room at least two times. I think it was in my head as I was thinking about sun salutations and also not wanting to leave in the middle of the practice. I didn't ever want to miss anything. It may have been a little OCD too.

It happened at night when I was little too. I would get in bed and the voices would start talking about needing to go to the bathroom once more. I would try to push them away but in the end I would get up, go, and come back to bed. Just easier that way so they would stop. As I got older, I was getting better at ignoring them and not having to go after going to bed. But not before yoga; they were insistent so I would just go.

I came back to my mat and started to move and stretch. It felt good to clear the cobwebs from my trip, plus with the time change, I was up the night before for the full moon converging with the sun rise. So far Hawaii was magical.

Now there were mats filling the waterfall room space. Catharine, our teacher arrived and stood in front of us, introduced herself to newcomers and began with the Anususara invocation chant followed by a themed story which would frame the practice. She was an Anusara teacher and that's how they started class. It was part of their training.

I liked to do that too but that was just part of me and how I connected to the practice, the students in my class and how I lived my life. Yoga, my teaching and my life were all threads that wove together. As Catharine spoke, I glanced around the space, Peter was next to me, and there were other men and women attentively and openly gazing at Catharine while she threaded the needle of the theme which would inspire us to go deeper inside for the inward journey during the practice.

Catharine was a knowledgeable guide and strong practitioner. She took us through a partner sequence and Peter and I were partnered up for the poses. It was a sequence leading us into visvamitrasana, an arm balance also known as flying warrior pose. This pose was not a part of my regular practice. It was kind of crazy and fun. I loved the partner assists. It was hard and made me laugh as Peter and I played in the poses.

After the partnering, we thanked each other and moved back to our individual space on our own mats. Into our hips, moving through a supine twist, we slowed and settled into svasana. I laid on my back in corpse pose with my legs out straight, feet relaxed and falling away from each other, arms down by my hips, palms open to receive. I felt someone close to my mat get up and felt the vacancy next to me.

In the space of a few moments, I heard the soft beginnings of a piano near me. I could feel the music coming from behind me and enveloping me in my own bubble in this waterfall room on my mat. Tears were streaming down my face as if right on cue to the melody I was hearing. I knew the yoga practice had softened me and now I was letting go. I didn't know what I was letting go of but I stayed with each tear as they slid down my cheeks. I laid in corpse pose and absorbed my practice and was carried and cared for by the music.

As the music slowed and gently stopped, I was amazed. I knew that music. I had played this in my yoga classes so many times and I had played this music during our daughter's labor while I was in the hospital. I had heard this style before.

Peter had been next to me. Peter had been the one to get up to play. This was Peter Kater. I wasn't a star struck person but what struck me was the strong connection to my life with yoga, my daughter, and how his music had influenced and gifted me in so many ways. This was no coincidence and was certainly a small miracle that I was happily acknowledging and thankful for.

After closing the practice with a revisit to the story, we bowed into our hearts with a Namaste. I opened my journal and began to write, tears once again streaming down my face. The music was incredibly healing and touched my heart deeply. It took me on a journey into myself to places that needed to be touched and opened. As I was writing, Peter came over to my mat and handed me a small cup of Kombucha. I thanked him for allowing me to join the retreat, our partner work, and the beautiful surprise of his playing.

I told him his gift of playing touched my soul. We chatted for a short time. He said he was having a concert that night with a couple of other musicians and to come, to bring my husband and our girls.

Ride Like the Wind

The essential joy of being with horses is that it brings us in contact with the rare elements of grace, beauty, spirit, and fire.

Sharon Ralls Lemon

Driving out in the beautiful hunt

country of Virginia, seeing the powerful horses, green pastures, and rolling hills, I got an idea.

I wanted to start riding.

I hadn't really been on a horse since Summer Camp and riding on the beach at Sea Island in the summers. The truth was I was afraid of horses. But there was always something that drew me to them.

While I was still married and living in D.C., I started driving an hour to Virginia hunt country and would ride for an hour or so. I would trail ride different horses each time, walking, trotting, and sometimes having them canter back to the barn with me. Some rides I would be terrified and other days it would feel so amazing and comfortable. Every time I would leave, I felt fulfilled, whole, and my soul had been nourished. I loved the horses, the smell of the saddle and the peacefulness of the trail. I talked to the horses and they talked back through their eyes and how it would feel when we were together on the trail or in the ring.

I wanted more.

I wanted to be at the barn everyday.

Riding was filling something in me.

I began taking lessons from a very patient trainer with the kindest black horse. I would groom him, saddle him, ride on the lunge line with no stirrups; building up my leg strength and hunt seat.

I re-learned everything from Summer Camp and improved my rusty skills.

I began to jump over small jumps.

Other things began to change in my life. I was happy at the barn. I felt a connection to myself I had never felt before. I would get nervous trying new things, like when I went to my first show, but I knew I could do it. I had more confidence and courage and wanted more. I felt like I was coming to life.

This was when I knew I would be okay if I left my marriage. Learning to do something that I was scared showed me that I could listen to my heart and be successful at something new. It didn't have to be perfect. I could do it.

I started working with my horse trainer and one of my best friends, Richard, at his barn to learn all I could about riding, to show, and do something new. I moved to Middleburg, Virginia, from D.C. to live in horse country. I stepped to a new edge I had never taken before.

Richard invited me into his life and into his love of horses.

Richard helped me find the perfect horse. A chestnut gelding, 16.2 hands, gorgeous, and "with chrome in all the right places," as Richard put it. He had white markings on his head and one leg near his hoof. Not too flashy and just enough to get a glance by someone walking by us in the practice ring at the horse show. Patrick. I called him Fat Pat.

He was perfect for me.

We were perfect for each other.

Something in my life was perfect.

In our conversations, Richard had built his friend Annette up to be celestial. He said she was beautiful, long legged, and the best horsewoman he knew. He said she was the nicest person he had ever met. Richard said I would learn a lot from her. He knew we would love each other, but to really make sure he told me it would be a good idea to bake Annette the zucchini bread I'd been making for him.

I baked it every time I went for a lesson. It was perfectly moist with shreds of zucchini and just enough crunchy on top to make your mouth salivate for more once a morsel hit your lips. He loved it and devoured it every time I brought it. He knew Annette would love it and it would make it easier for her to say yes to me bringing Fat Pat to board at her barn, Grand View Farm. Richard said it would make a nice thoughtful touch and good impression. Richard always paid attention to detail; sometimes over the top.

He didn't exaggerate. When we drove up to the barn pulling my silver Kingston two horse trailer with Fat Pat inside, I saw her standing next to the barn with her hands on her forehead shading her face from the sun. Her mane was chestnut just like my horse! Beautiful red hair to her mid-back, mile long legs, and an inviting smile.

Annette and I hit it off from the introduction. When you meet someone and you feel like you've known each other forever, it fits just like a puzzle piece to a 1,000 piece puzzle where all the colors are so similar but you just know you've got the right piece when you pick it up and before it even lands in the spot you've planned for it. I knew I was in the right place.

We fit.

The barn at her farm was an old-fashioned red barn with a hay loft above and a wallpaper of hay bales on both the back and front sides. Each stall was cleaned and freshly picked. Each horse impeccably spoiled and cared for, groomed and brushed with shiny coats and all of them looking at the stall doors as we walked through the barn aisle. It wasn't a huge, fancy show barn, like Woodhall where I went for lessons with Richard. It had character and richness that I felt in the warmth of the horses' whinnies as I petted each one at their stall door and fed them carrots.

Back to the trailer to unload Fat Pat and lead him to the large stall on the right. We were home. The piece fit perfectly. He walked in, sniffed every corner, sipped from his water bucket, and then rolled in the middle of the stall in the fresh shavings perfectly combed and fluffed for him.

I felt his smile as he looked at me when he rolled upright to standing. He went to his hay and began to munch.

I had a new horse, a new barn, and a new friendship with Annette.

Annette suggested giving Fat Pat a day to settle in to his new stall and the farm. She would turn him out in the paddock most of the next day. I planned to come out in the afternoon after work. Annette's fourteen-year-old daughter, Leslie, and I would trail ride on the farm to take things slow and let him get used to the farm. There were cows on the farm in the back pasture. We would ride through there and around the farm.

I groomed him and tacked him up as I got myself ready to ride. Richard was insistent upon a few things, one of them being that you showed up to ride looking groomed yourself. That meant polished and shined paddock boots, shirt tucked in to jeans wearing a belt, hair in a hairnet and helmet, even if you weren't showing.

Although some days I opted out of the helmet because I wasn't jumping and so I just wore a baseball cap.

Today I wore a helmet because the farm was new territory to me and Fat Pat. And I was starting to see Annette had a worry bone in her and I knew it made her feel more comfortable too. It was a lot of responsibility running a farm and having a family.

Fat Pat was saddled, poised and ready and so was I, per Richard's riding etiquette. Leslie was riding her horse,

Image. We walked out through the gate and into the field just past the cows.

I quickly learned Fat Pat was not a huge fan of cows but he did well and I was able to move him forward past them and onto our ride. I just kept thinking, *How did I get so lucky to be here, to be riding Fat Pat who was a stunner and so sweet, to meet Annette and her family?*

It was perfect timing. I needed this distraction from my life. I needed this to be my life. The sun was shining with just the right amount of warmth. The hills were green with longish grasses capped with tiny yellow flowers swaying in the light breeze. As we walked over them, there were pops and clicks that must have been some sort of grasshopper getting out of the way of the massive horse hooves coming their direction.

I was paying attention on the ride because it was our first ride on the farm. I alertly absorbed every detail as it could be important. We walked along and came up to a small ditch with some water running through it. Not much water at all but enough that Fat Pat crow hopped over it as if it was the Grand Canyon; his back arched and his legs stiffened. We landed on the other side after our elevated flight.

I took a double take to make sure I was still in the saddle and not all catawampus up on his neck. Leslie was laughing, but behind the laughter I could see her eyes were as big as dinner plates. I think she felt a sense of responsibility to keep us safe and get us back to the barn in one piece.

I could see her mom in her; the strong protector and a bit of a worrier but in a good caring way, not a nagging foreboding or controlling way. It was a sweet endearing quality that I could deal with because she meant well and it felt like caring mixed with safety instead of insecurity mixed with jealousy.

I knew all this already because I was a keen observer and it was right there. I could see Annette's mama bear qualities and I admired and respected that in her. Annette was not surface. She was a bit shy, but that passed quickly as we both felt an instant kinship toward each other. We could just be ourselves with each other.

So refreshing to be myself with a woman.

For so much in my life, I was on guard to protect myself. In my experiences so far, women were not nice. They were jealous, petty, and didn't want you to have it even if they didn't want it. Always a competition. I always had to be watching for this because I didn't want to not feel in control and something bad happen. Annette was different.

I realize I'm not catawampus after the unexpected jump and straighten my back tall, butt deep in the saddle, heels down, and legs slightly forward just in case Fat Pat decides he thinks he's a green two-year-old again at the Belmont race track instead of in his nine-year-old thoroughbred gelding body with occasional ouchy achiness in his right front fetlock.

Leslie and I walk on together with our steeds. Just as we're cresting the hill, I can hear Highway 66 in the near distance, reminding me that I'm still near and in my old life. Fat Pat's ears prick up and his whole body lifts to alert status. I feel every muscle in his 1,200 pound frame tense.

Shit.

We whip around and Patrick leaps into a full gallop.

No walk to trot to canter to gallop. We skipped the first three gaits and are full throttle at bolt. I don't look behind to see where Leslie is because I'm too focused on holding on and pulling the reins back to stop him but I hear hooves pounding behind me. Image must have bolted too.

Funny and not funny how horses can hear something a mile away that sends them to the moon, or maybe it was those crickets jumping in the grass. No matter now, I've got to stop him before I fall off or we both get hurt. Were they sure he wasn't fast enough to be a race horse because I'm thinking right now we have a chance at winning.

Shit.

It's like summer camp one year, when I lost control of

my horse and he took off on the trail. This time I know what to do and it's not working. How can a bridle and a D-ring snaffle bit really stop him now? It's not. Maybe we should have used a stronger bit? Too late now.

I can see a wire fence up ahead and we're headed straight for it. I wonder if Fat Pat sees it. Will we jump it? Will he run into it and hurt himself?

I've got to pull back harder. I press my heels down more, sit back and butt deep, and pull not just with my hands but with my arms, legs, and my whole being. I focus and visualize a ray of my thought to Stop Now, hitting his brain talking mind to mind and willing him to stop for his own good and mine too.

As I get closer, I still can barely see the wire.

Does he see it?

Does he sense it?

Bam! He lands all four feet on the ground at one time as if a helicopter just lowered us to that exact spot. We are stopped. We are stopped a foot from the wire fence. His nostrils are flaring with every rapid breath he takes. His body is heavily pulsing underneath me. My heart is racing outside of me as it's broken the barrier from inside its cavity to the world outside of green, blue and light brown dust particles flying around us.

He stopped.

He stopped.

He stopped.

Thank God. Just as I was giving thanks and recovering myself, I remembered Leslie and as I look back to see where she was, she and Image land beside me in second place. We shared a quick glance and knew we were okay.

"What in the hell happened", I asked her.

"I have no idea, you took off on Fat Pat and then Image took off and I couldn't stop her," she said.

We both started laughing. I was still shaking. I knew it would be okay but my body was still in fight or flight mode. We did our best to walk slowly back to the barn. Fat Pat was still spooky but we made it. So much for a leisurely trail ride on our first day out. We have bonded. I love him. I love our new home.

Fat Pat and I got to know each other better in our lessons with Richard, ring rides, trails, and showing. And I got to know Richard too.

Richard had been riding since he was single digits and it was just a part of who he was. It was his life. While he loved the horses, there seemed to be a part that he also resented. He was an excellent trainer but sometimes the anger inside him welled up and came out in a big way. This I had been around before. I knew how to dodge it but it still didn't feel good.

When he would yell at me while I was riding, I froze, and my mind would go someplace else just like when I was little. It was like I couldn't think or do anything. I was just there and not there. One time Fat Pat and I had a lesson with Richard. I could not get this one jump right; either I was getting it short or way too long. It was a sharp right turn to a short approach to the jump. I couldn't get the turn so the jump was too long or too short.

Fat Pat and I must have done the jump fifty times. I felt so bad for Fat Pat because it was my fault. Annette came out when she saw what was happening. She knew it was time to stop. She gave Richard the eye and stood there so we stopped. I need repetition to learn (not that much) but I also needed space to feel safe. If not, I was not all there. I couldn't think straight.

There were many moments like this for me with Richard but there were also moments of deep friendship that developed as we grew to have a deep caring for each other. Nothing would ever go further than friendship because Richard was gay.

I knew that and it felt safe to be his friend. I was still married even if it wasn't happily. I didn't feel comfortable having male friends. I was married. Men always came onto me. I had a hard time standing up for myself so I would do my best to ignore it, walk away or laugh it off. Richard was safe in that way for me. He was funny, generous and kind. He had an anger streak that came out sometimes but not always.

After my divorce, when I moved to Middleburg, Richard and I became very close. We loved each other but he was gay. We had planned that if I didn't meet someone and get married, he and I would get married. We even told our friends in the horse world, we were getting married.

I liked that. It felt safe. We loved hanging out going to movies, being with the horses, and going to shows. He could be moody at times but his heart meant well. I knew when he was hard on me in my riding lessons that he still cared for me. I did my best not to take it personally but sometimes it was hard.

I did love him. I loved him differently than in a physical way. I knew that wasn't possible so once I put that out of my head and heart, I was okay. He also said he would have a baby with me if I wanted to have children. I didn't even know if I wanted to be married again, or for that matter, have children. I was just getting over my divorce.

Richard seemed like a good start. It was fun and free. No sex of course but I didn't need that anyway. Not then anyway. We agreed if we did get married, that it would be okay if we had physical partners. I didn't need it then so I didn't think about it.

Until I met someone, and so did Richard. Richard met Josh.

I met this someone and slept with him the first night I met him. We met at the horse show at Madison Square Garden. It was one of the top horse shows on the circuit. I wasn't showing, but one of Richard's clients was showing. I was helping and watching the show.

One night after showing, a lot of us decided to go out dancing at a club. Lots of drinks, close dancing, and knowing glances of what was possible and a foretelling of what would happen. The next morning, Richard asked, "Did you sleep with him?" Not because he was mad.

Because he knew if I did sleep with him, I was just a notch in this person's belt. I meant nothing.

I tried to push away the voices and say, "I'm different, I think he really likes me." We did end up seeing each other a few times traveling to several beaches to have a rendezvous. I wanted more. I tried to make him my "boyfriend" or maybe it was I was trying to make him into my "husband" now. I was following my pattern. It's what I thought I needed to be happy and safe.

As much as I was working through the settling around my divorce and starting my new life, I still had the collisions inside occasionally. I could do so well for a long time, not drinking, working, riding, and doing my new life.

Then I would feel it. Still some doubt rolling around. Was I good enough? Would I ever meet someone again? What went so wrong in my marriage and why did I even get married in the first place?

I had reconciled and let go of so much. I had done a lot of praying. I had forgiven myself for so much. Why did my craziness have to come up still? Was I crazy? I don't think so but I didn't feel completely normal either. What was normal?

I had found a family in Richard and Josh, Annette, and her daughter, Leslie. I felt so happy with Fat Pat. I loved riding. I felt more confident in my life than I could remember. It was like I was going so great for a while and I sabotaged my life with drinking binges. It was as if I was waiting for the other shoe to drop.

Everything was going great.

Then it wasn't.

I was going to visit the guy I met at Madison Square Garden; we'd been seeing each other every couple of months. No strings, just casual get togethers even though I wanted more. I did my best to let that go. We were meeting in Palm Beach in a few weeks. I was feeling great about myself. I was happy riding,

My showing was coming along and I was feeling more accomplished as a horsewoman. I was feeling happy with everything. I was also feeling more ready to look at the possibility that I did want to meet a man and have that kind of life again. I didn't want to force it. I thought maybe this man I was meeting would be that man. I felt positive and hopeful.

Then I did it.

One night I went to the theatre in D.C. with two girlfriends. It was a great show but we wanted to stay out longer and do something fun. We started driving around town. We spotted a convertible with three guys. They spotted us too. We stopped, chatted, climbed in their car and drove to their house for a party.

We had been drinking and wanted more. We listened to music, snorted coke, and as the night drew on, smoked a joint. There was no kissing or intimacy at all, just talking, drinking, and drugs. As morning came, we were still high and took a cab to my car. I drove us home, dropped my friends off, and drove to the store for some beer. I needed to level out. I was still coked up. The pot did not help me come down. I felt very amped up, more than I thought I should be. Something was different about this high. On the drive home, I drank a couple of beers. It was slowly bringing me to a level place.

I got home to "the mouse house", a cottage on an estate in Middleburg, Virginia, where I lived with Richard and Josh. They were both away at horse shows. I was by myself. The sun was shining. I parked the car, walked upstairs, and passed out. I woke up in the late afternoon. I was sick but not throwing up. My head was heavy as a rock and I couldn't lift it above my waist as I walked to the bathroom. I hadn't eaten and had tacky gums from the cocaine.

I remembered this feeling from college but this was worse. I thought I needed to go to the hospital but I didn't want to chance it. What had I smoked? Was something in the joint with the pot? I was crying on the floor unable to get up, beating myself up again. Why did I do this again? Everything was going so well? What was wrong with me?

Why couldn't I stop? Where did this collision come from and why?

I cried for Josh. I cried for Richard. I needed them to come home. I needed help.

I couldn't call Annette. I didn't want her to think I was bad. Growing up, her Dad had been an alcoholic so she didn't drink. We had talked about our childhoods before with Mom being a drinker and her Dad being a drinker. Annette knew I drank some, but this would be too much.

I sweated it out. I crawled downstairs to get some water. I tried to eat some crackers thinking it would help. I slept on the kitchen floor for a while. It was cold. It wasn't moving. I was still. I would be okay. God, make it okay and I won't do it again.

I woke in the middle of the night on the kitchen floor. I ate a few more crackers and made my way upstairs. I folded myself into bed. Josh and Richard would be home tomorrow. I'm going to be okay.

Don't Go

Life shrinks or expands in proportion to one's courage.

Anais Nin

Dad left Mom for the first time when

I was nine or ten. I remember him leaving that day. I don't remember him packing or telling Mom but I do remember him saying goodbye to Brother and me. He hugged us and said goodbye in the living room. He started to walk out the front door.

Mom was sobbing and begging him not to leave. I remember seeing her holding on to him and trying to pull him back into the house. I remember her falling and holding on to his leg as he was out in the driveway trying to get in his car.

I felt her desperation, her heart's aching, and the tears on her face matched the tears on mine. My lips quivered and the tears poured down into my mouth and down my neck. Brother stood next to me and I could feel his hand in mine but I could only see what was directly in front of me.

Dad was leaving.

He was leaving us.

He was leaving me.

I didn't really know why he was leaving except that I knew they had been fighting a lot and Mom was drinking a lot more. Dad was gone a lot, working and golf trips, so they weren't spending much time together.

Dad had an apartment at the Chateaux Apartments and Brother and I could come and spend the night with him whenever we wanted. He had all new furniture and a room for me and Brother too. It was a little uncomfortable at first because we weren't used to spending so much time alone with Dad, but then it was okay.

Mom was really mad and would talk about Dad to me. She said she thought he had a girlfriend and that's why he left us. I remember thinking about both Mom and Dad and why this had happened. Being with Mom and Dad was like being on a tightrope. I walked carefully in the middle between them. I understood both sides. I understood that Mom was lonely and sad and that's why she drank. She wanted Dad to spend more time with her and not work and golf so much. She wanted him to tell her she was pretty and bring her flowers. She wanted to feel special and that she mattered.

I also got how Dad would get so mad. He would come home and Mom had been drinking and it would progress through the night. When she would get really upset after we'd all gone to bed, she would wake up Dad and start yelling at him. Sometimes it got really bad and I would lock my door and put a pillow over my ears. I got why they were both upset and I didn't understand why they couldn't talk and just fix it.

Our family wasn't very good at resolution.

Dad is a smart and powerful attorney and the law is about resolution. Can he do this at home too? We stuffed things under the rug in our family and didn't have family conversations to talk about anything.

Mom took care of things.

Dad took care of things.

Rarely did it seem they took care of things together. The lack of knowing how to discuss, compromise, or even bring things out in the open. We just didn't do that. As long as it looked perfect on the outside, it was okay to just keep going. This was a generational pattern that I now see.

I became a stuffer. I stuffed things in my closet I didn't want to wear. I stuffed my feelings deep down inside that I knew we weren't supposed to talk about out loud. My outside world of stuffing was reflecting my inner world of stuffing, denial, isolation, fear and unworthiness.

I had noticed Mom's sadness. I noticed Dad didn't come home for lunch anymore like he did when I was little.

I remember Dad driving into the driveway and Mom so happy to see him. She made good lunches and had it all ready for him when he got home. This made her happy to see him happy. Then Dad started working more at the law firm. Mom would iron while watching "Days of Our Lives" with the hourglass at the beginning while my nanny played games with me in my room.

I loved it when Dad came home too. It was a special surprise when Dad came home at lunch and I knew it meant he loved us.

Dad got home in the afternoons around 5 o'clock. He wore a suit and tie every day to work. When he got home Mom, had started dinner and was back sitting on the couch, needlepointing, and watching TV. He would kiss Mom. We would run to say hi. He would go downstairs to where he kept his clothes and got dressed everyday. He would put on some clothes so he could come and relax. He would maybe fix a drink, but it seemed my parents were more social on the weekends.

Walk Like an Egyptian

*And forget not that the earth delights to feel your bare feet
and the winds long to play with your hair.*

Kahlil Gibran

I couldn't believe my parents actually said "Yes!"

I'm going to Egypt for three weeks with my friend
Rema Mixon and her family. Mom and Dad were
concerned about the occurrence of political upheaval in
Egypt due to the controversy surrounding Anwar Sadat,
President of Egypt and his visit to Jerusalem, and the
repercussions in Egypt while I was there visiting. Rema's
grandfather, Salah Farid was Egyptian and was an
Ambassador of the Arab League. Both he and Rema's
mother assured them I would be fine and we would be able
to talk with them by phone for check-ins.

I was twelve. Awkward, knobby knees, tall, size 9 feet,
buck teeth, self-conscious, and begging for adventure. That
coming school year, I was leaving St. Mary's and going to
Darlington Middle School.

Growing up in Rome, Georgia, meant I knew almost everyone at the grocery store or when we went to lunch at Huff's. Pete, the owner of the Texaco gas station, knew our name, pumped our gas, and charged it to Dad. I had some of the same teachers at Darlington School that Mom and Dad had when they were in school. There wasn't a lot of anonymity.

Rome was safe.

I walked up our half circle driveway to check the mailbox every day to see if my passport had arrived.

I wanted so badly to go on this trip with Rema and to ride a camel in Egypt. I knew about the pyramids, King Tut, and camels.

I didn't feel nervous at all about traveling this far from my parents. This wasn't all that different than going to Camp Juliette Lowe for Summer Camp for two weeks or a month at a time; I was comfortable being away from my family. It was a welcome break from the unpredictable temperament of the goings on at home.

The day before I was to leave, my passport arrived in the mail.

All was arranged, packing done, outfit planned for the plane, and a large glass jar of Jiff peanut butter in my carry on, just in case. I sat in aisle 31 on our Delta flight to New York. We would then transfer to Pakistan Airlines to Cairo with a brief stops in Paris and Frankfurt. It was the most time I'd ever traveled by plane.

We arrived in New York and learned of a 7 hour layover delay we weren't expecting. Rema and I got moments to stretch our long young legs and ran around in the airport with her brother, Ron. In a moment of silly play, Ron grabbed my carry on and accidentally dropped it. I heard the ping thump of the Jiff jar breaking in my bag.

Mrs. Mixon told me later that she was looking at my face in that moment and she said I was pitiful and it looked as though "I had lost my connection to home."

The jar wasn't salvageable. No big deal to some, but to me the difference between eating and not eating. Jiff had been my lifeline, my security that I wouldn't go hungry.

I felt my independence outwardly shining while arranging my seat area on the plane. All easily accessible for the flight: book in its place, pillow and blanket set. We even were asked over the speaker to read our menus in the seat back pocket. The stewardess would be coming to take our order for dinner, lunch, and snacks. For dinner I chose "shrimp cocktail, fillet mignon of Texas Beef, mushroom sauce, duchess potatoes, string beans almandine, pineapple cheesecake, cheese and crackers" and water. For lunch, "shrimp cocktail, escalope of beef marsala, noisette potatoes, buttered peas franchise, grilled tomato, mandarin surprise and cheese and crackers" and more water.

I saved the menus for my scrapbook.

I felt respected and fancy. Rema and I had promised to take in every moment of the trip together, saving boarding passes, menus, brochures and taking lots of photos.

I've known Rema since we were four years old. Her entire family was my adopted family. I knew them all, visited with them at Christmas, and spent the night a lot. We were best friends. Rema's mom was the French teacher at Darlington Middle School and drove me to school every day from 7th grade until I turned 16.

I would walk through the woods to their house every morning at 7 am. She would drive us to school in her car, Charlie, while drinking coffee and putting on her mascara. She had the muscle strength in her arms to pull it all off even though Charlie had no power steering.

Mrs. Mixon, as I still call her, was strong-willed, persistent, and resourceful. She spoke French, Arabic and English. She meant business and you knew it because she would start talking in French or Arabic when she wanted to impress a point. This means pay attention, even if you don't know what she's saying. She was also one of the kindest women who could do anything she sets out to do.

I trusted her and her parents to be there for us on this trip.

We arrived at the Farid's flat, located on the island of

Zamalek in the middle of the city of Cairo. Mrs. Mixon had grown up in this flat with her parents and their servants, Gamalat and Abdou. They were both there to greet us upon our arrival after several long flights.

Gamalat is translated as "the pretty one" and when we met her, she was an older woman with gray hair and a slight stoop so you didn't see her face much unless she sat and looked up at you. She had a quiet inner beauty outwardly expressed through her dedicated rituals of cooking and cleaning at the flat.

Abdou was, as Mrs. Mixon shared with me, "black as the ace of spades." His title was chauffeur and butler but he was known for keeping everything in order and taking care of their every need when she grew up here.

Her parents, the Farids, opened their home to me, invited me in like I was one of them. I felt their warm welcome and acceptance from all of their family as they greeted me with a kiss on both cheeks. I repeated the ritual with them. I had never kissed so much, or so many people, in my life and it felt a little funny, but at the same time specialness flooded my heart. I felt a belonging.

The flat was on the ground floor. It was airy, spacious, and each room had shuttered windows and doors onto the garden patio framed with lush plants which offered shade to the space outside and within. Each morning, very early around 4:30 or 5 am, Gamalat would wash the concrete tile patio and the shutters with cool water. I would hear the clink of her setting down her bucket on the concrete floor, dipping the towel in the water, wringing it out and swishing it around in a semi-circle motion to clean the tile and then wiping the shutters side to side. The repeated sounds of conscious caring would go on for what felt like hours. It lured me into a deep meditative state of peace and gratitude for her devotion and pride. I would sometimes peek outside to see her movements in the bits of morning light that shone on her as if she was betrothed to the ritual.

The food was in no way like the food I had eaten before. My food choices in life had been tacos, spaghetti, traditional holiday dinners, steak, TV dinners, and fast food.

I was a picky eater and the peanut butter was gone. They did have Wimpy Burger, but the hamburgers were made from water buffalo and just knowing that and then tasting them, I couldn't eat it.

We did have one meal that I loved for a couple of reasons. First, the restaurant was under a big tent like a white wedding tent and there were thousands of cats all around us begging for scraps. I loved animals, especially cats, and I was in heaven. I was told not to pet them or feed them but I would sneak my hand under the table to give them a little rub on their ears. I wanted to take some home so badly.

The reason there were so many cats hanging around was because it was a restaurant that served squab. Yes, pigeon typically under four weeks old. It was so good. It was like eating chicken but much better. I ate until my belly was sore and sticking out. I ate thinking that I could make up for lost meals and prepare ahead for missed future meals.

The other thing that was very tasty to eat was the Salbia, which were similar to our donut holes. There were big pots of boiling oil in a giant tin drum on the side of the road where vendors would fry these clumps of batter, dump them on paper on the table, and roll them in a glaze. Those I could eat.

Eating was a not my priority and if anything, I avoided it. I still kept an observant eye out for something I could eat but my focus was elsewhere.

Everything was so different in this country from what I knew and there was so much to absorb. What I realized was this was an immense privilege to experience the culture, the people, the open air markets, and this whole trip with a family who lived there. Being on a tour and traveling would have been a completely different experience.

For the three weeks I was in Egypt, I was a local.

Rema's grandfather, Salah, took us to the local markets where we saw the men congregating and smoking their hookahs, he bargained for gold bracelets for me to take home to Mom as a gift, and we saw mourners all wearing black in a funeral procession walking through town as they carried the casket and cried and wailed for their loss. There was so much happening in the marketplace with vendors cooking open air in the streets and smells of sweets and sausages mingling together in the air we walked through, meat hanging from hooks, vegetables for sale, jewelry, colorful scarves and belly dancing outfits, people arguing, and dogs running in the street. It appeared a normal day with the rhythms of their words, crying, singing, smells as they all moved with each other.

I felt a palpable energy of excitement and organized chaos.

I'll have to admit the trip had been a bit surreal so far. I had never been out of the country before and had only been to Florida and Alabama. Egypt was certainly far from the South where I grew up.

I was still sticking to my not eating anything that didn't look familiar or like it tasted good so I wasn't eating much of anything. I was starting to feel a little weak, but I was determined. I had control over my body and no one could tell me what to do. In a way it felt good to have this control.

On the other hand I was just hungry.

This trip was non-stop excitement as we had so many things planned it kept me from thinking too much about food and the jar of lost peanut butter.

We went to a mosque and to the Egyptian Museum in Cairo where we saw King Tut. It all felt very old, smelled musty, and felt as if we were on a dig for treasure.

We planned to spend some time at the flat in Cairo, do some sightseeing, meet family and tour, then we were going to the beach in Alexandria. There they had a small day beach cabana for us to hang out, swim, and play in the waves. I was told that the beach cabana was just down the beach from Anwar Sadat's beach house and Omar Shariff's beach cabana. Before I left for my trip, Nannie told me Sadat was the President of Egypt and Omar Shariff, was a very famous, handsome actor from the movie Doctor Zhivago.

One night we were home alone at the flat and we were emphatically told to stay in the flat no matter what happened. We heard a loud sound like a gunshot. We were so scared that we ran to the doorman. We were in our nightgowns; a huge no no in the culture.

The doormen didn't speak English well. There were armed guards outside. We were escorted into the flat and told to stay put. When everyone got home that night, we were scolded and told never to do that again.

It scared me; I didn't want to get in trouble.

Unpredictable Beauty

It is never too late to be who you might have been.

George Eliot

I was invited to my friend Deanna's

wedding and I was waffling whether I should go or not. This was my first wedding to attend since my own. I had turned down wedding invites from close friends because I was still too raw and feeling too much pain from the divorce.

When I was getting divorced I looked up friends who lived far away that I might visit. Deanna was living with John in San Francisco. I called and asked if I could come. I flew out and was so grateful to stay with them for a long weekend. I even was introduced to one of their friends, Luke. We said our "hellos" but I wasn't ready yet, still going through the healing and sorting through my divorce.

A year later, I was more ready with a knowing that I did not want to get hurt again. This time, I was ready. Rema called me and invited me to stay with her at the Ritz Carlton Hotel in Amelia Island and go to the wedding. I decided to get a ticket and meet her there. I was honestly excited to see John and Deanna marry.

We arrived at Amelia Island on the Thursday before the wedding for a pre-party with the wedding party and other guests flying in early. Destination weddings meant possible hook ups, parties, dressing up, beach, and too much fun. It was nice to have a break and some fun with friends after the divorce. Rema and I had a few cocktails on the club level at the Ritz and then drove to the party at Deanna's condo.

Deanna and John's families were there. We met so many of John's friends from California including Luke, the man I had met in San Francisco when I visited John and Deanna just a year earlier. Luke and I were instantly magnetized to each other when we were reintroduced.

Luke fixed me a gin and tonic in a large red plastic tumbler cup and we talked nonstop and ate M&M's until everyone decided to leave. I went with Rema and he went with the rest of the groomsmen. Immediately, I felt a pull toward him, coupled with a pang of fear. I don't want to get hurt anymore and I'm not sure I even want a relationship.

During my time in Virginia, living with my friends Josh and Richard, I came to the conclusion that I may never want to marry again and that felt safe and right. I wanted to be self-sufficient in every way. I decided to have a good time over the weekend with no expectations and at the same time I could feel the voices in my mind, "You never know what's possible unless you open up again."

Close.

Open.

Contraction.

Expansion.

Let life air out Camden and see what blows in.

Ok, I can do that.

During this weekend of their wedding was the funeral service for Princess Diana. She was killed on August 31, 1997 and her service was to be broadcast on TV very early the morning of September 6th, the day of John and

Deanna's wedding.

That Friday night, after running the pool tables at the Palace Saloon together and lots of dancing, Luke and I headed back to the Ritz. I kissed him first in the hallway to my room. My roommates were gone so we spent the night together. He was romantic, caring, kind, open, and attentive.

I was nervous so I reminded myself of my intention, "Let life air out Camden and see what blows in."

Just have fun.

Don't get attached.

Stay protected.

I was doing my best to be in the middle place and not think right away, *this man is the answer to my prayers and my dream is coming true.*

Rema and her friend had come in late night or early morning and were in the bed next to us. She set her alarm so we could watch Princess Diana's funeral service. Luke was sound asleep, and Rema looked over and gave me the look of "How did he get here?"

I shrugged. I didn't need to explain; I was having fun, don't get attached, guard my heart.

We watched the service and quietly mourned the loss of a life of hope, risk, compassion, and possibility. Elton John sang "Candle in the Wind". It was time to buckle my seat belt to the wild abandon of a new adventure. After the service, we slept a few more hours and woke around 10 am. Luke took the "walk of shame". This was not a bad thing for him or me, especially when his friends saw him and knew he had a conquest with a divorcee, as John called me.

I was happy to spend time with him. I was opening doors and not attached.

It was the wedding day and since Luke was the best man, he was busy with festivities. I sat by the pool with friends. I thought about him and our night together. I wondered if it would happen again. Did I want it to happen again?

Have fun. Don't be attached. Protect my heart.

The wedding was beautiful and so fun. The weather wasn't humid which was great; 100% humidity with scorching temperatures was common. With my curly hair, I was thankful it was tamed and coiffed. I was excited for our friends and I was excited to see Luke after the wedding. Champagne was flowing at the reception and servers were taking drink orders to a full bar. I had my eye on Luke across the room very nonchalantly. I quickly glanced away after a shy smile as he caught my eye. I decided to play a game. I would walk to the other side of the room and see if he would come my way. I made my way across and found my station. He followed. I did this a couple more times and decided he was committed to another talk at least. I was elated.

Maybe this was still bargaining with myself or playing games, but I decided it was a good way to see where he landed with our time together. We enjoyed a quick embrace and kiss and then he dropped a surprise on me, "I'd like to introduce you to my parents and family."

Wow, this was soon and I'd had several cocktails already but he insisted. I met his parents, Sam and Sue, and his sister Stephanie. I thought this must be a sign that he did like me. Life was feeling flirty and fun. I was at the single table, he was at the wedding head table.

His sister often tells a story that reminds me of our sweet beginnings. "I watched Luke watching you walk to your table, his mouth open, smile on his face and his eyes fixed on you as you walked to your table and sat down. I knew he was in love."

Luke had a second "walk of shame" the next morning. We didn't exchange numbers. We kissed and said goodbye. That was the end and the beginning.

The voices started up again…

Why did you sleep with him, he won't call you now.

Is this what you want for your life.

You shouldn't have done that, Camden.

I pushed them aside; in this new chapter of my life, I vowed to have more awareness of my decisions. I was going to express what I needed in a relationship and not just do what kept the peace. My process would be to first check in to see how I felt.

Luke called a few days later. He called the mother of the bride and got my phone number. My heart was squeezed by this gesture, seemingly so simple, but it delivered a walloping confirmation to my new independent life that when you tell yourself you matter and act like it, you do matter.

He invited me to Sausalito, California where I had met him briefly just a year before. I said yes to a visit in two weeks. It was September and Indian Summer, epic weather for my trip.

I saw something different in Luke. His eyes were trusting. His hands were kind. He brought out something in me that felt good. I started to trust my feelings and hear my intuition again. I was adamant about not changing my life for a man again.

We started dating. We were dating long distance. He was living in California. I was living in Virginia. and after a month we knew that we were in love. I was ready for a move. I was ready for something new in my life; I had been in the Virginia area for ten years and was ready to say yes to that next leap.

At the same time of being excited and enthused I was also terrified, but I wasn't paralyzed anymore. I wasn't paralyzed by the fear and the doubt and the unworthiness. I was intrigued by the possibility of new adventures.

I decided to move California.

The big joke with Luke and his friends was that he knew I was serious about moving because my horse, George, arrived before I did. He shipped out with Johnson Horse Transportation and arrived in Woodside, CA a few weeks before me and Wally, my dog. Wally was my best friend and protector. I left my family in Virginia: my roommates Richard and Josh, my best friend Annette who honestly put herself out there and told me to move and give this new life a chance as much as she didn't want me to go.

Annette had met Luke when he came to visit me in Virginia and said he was different than anyone I had dated. He had kind eyes and she felt he cared for me with a loving heart. She said, "Don't go down the same path and be with the same type of guy like the one you've been with over and over. You'll marry, have children, he'll cheat and leave. That's not good enough for you. You've got to give Luke a chance but don't build your life around him, make a life for yourself. Take Wally and George, they'll take care of you and go explore something new. I'll always be here for you."

I needed to have something of my own so bringing my horse to California was a huge source of happiness, confidence, and independence for me. I started showing horses. Fat Pat didn't make the trip to California with me because his front fetlock was too sore. He retired and was happy staying at Annette's living the leisure life.

I bought a new horse, Asbury Park, but he went by his barn name, George. When he and I arrived and settled, I started going to horse shows with him. We got some high score ribbons and most importantly, we were a team.

George understood me and took care of me. One friend and trainer, who knew George for many years and had seen him show with several different riders, told me he saw George do things in the riding ring with me he had never seen him do for any other rider before. He said he was amazed at how he really took care of me, he'd never seen anything like it. That made me smile.

When George and I had a good ride, it was like we were flying. Our rhythm was smooth, matched perfectly and we were in sync.

I had such a good time at the barn and at shows and I loved the women who rode at the barn with me. It was nice and smart to have my own thing.

I made a vow to myself:

I'm not moving for another person only. If this doesn't work out with him, I have gained insight, I've gained excitement, I've gained adventure, and I've gained something new in my life that has enriched me and that has opened a new part of me to living more fully, to living more courageously and to saying yes.

A recording that played on repeat in my thoughts was Mom saying "You better marry a rich man if you want to live like you do."

I knew when I moved, I needed something of my own so I didn't want to be needy or dependent on Luke. It was time to build my life. It was time to figure some things out.

During my first year in California I realized I couldn't depend on anybody else to make me happy. It wasn't their job. It was my responsibility to love myself first.

I met Luke's brother, Mike, who introduced me to the concept of spirituality. I learned that religion was different than spirituality; I could be religious and spiritual and I also could be spiritual but not belong to a religion. I decided the latter was me.

I learned about compassion. I learned not just defense mechanisms in living my life and coping but I learned ways to actually process and work through things so I could respond and not react and put up walls.

Luke would always tell me how beautiful I was. I would look down at the ground and away from him. I wouldn't accept the compliment. I was uncomfortable and had that muskrat lump in my throat again and tears were even forming in my eyes. Where he really pushed the limit, was when he asked me to say "I am beautiful." I couldn't do it. I wouldn't do it.

I still had this child inside of me that felt stupid, that felt ugly with buck teeth, that felt awkward, that felt like I stood out, that felt like sometimes I still wanted to suck my thumb which I had not given up until 5th grade. I needed some padding and protection to hide me.

Luke was grounded, calm and cautious. I was a dreamer and jumped in many times without thinking or just wanting to take control and do it my way. His reflection of my own inner beauty gave me a glimpse into myself that I had not wanted to see before.

Innocence

We are born of love; Love is our mother.

Rumi

I met another boy I liked. He was a sophomore and I was a freshman. He was so cute, smart, and nice. He was a little shy, like me, but he had a lot of friends too. We had a lot in common, including that our grandparents knew each other because they were both in the cotton mill business. They had known each other a long time. Our parents knew each other too, but were more like acquaintances.

Cooper and I started hanging out at school. We talked on the phone for hours at a time at night. Dad said I wasn't allowed to date but Cooper could come to the house if we wanted to spend time together. He would come over and watch movies. We would sit in the den while my parents stayed in their bedroom and watched TV. Cooper would hold my hand sometimes; once Dad walked in and saw us. Cooper pulled his hand away quickly. I think he was afraid of Dad.

The Winter Dance was coming up. Cooper asked me to go. I really wanted to go but I knew I wasn't yet allowed to date. I would be fourteen on January 13 and it was still December.

Deep breath.

Ask my parents.

They had a multitude of questions:

Who would be driving us? Where was the dance? What time did it start and end?

I was a good daughter and got all the information they requested. We would be going with Michael and Susan. They were older and very responsible; Michael would drive us in his Granada. The dance was over at eleven o'clock.

Mom and Dad agreed and the terms were clear: Cooper was to come to the door, ring the bell and pick me up for the dance. There was to be no drinking. I had to be home right after the dance, by 11:30.

I could do that! I was floating I was so excited. My first dance. I had to pick the perfect outfit. I was not very close friends with Susan and Michael. They were older and seemed nice when I had been around them at school in the student lounge. My friends and I laughed about me going to the dance in a Granada. Not the coolest car, but I was going to the dance at least.

I spent time getting ready, making sure I felt good about my outfit, my hair, and I had the night planned out in my head. Cooper and I had been talking about how much fun we were going to have. I heard the Granada drive up in our driveway. I hovered at the door to my room. The bell rang. Dad walked to the door and opened it, "Hi Cooper, it's good to see you."

"Hi, Mr. Jones, good to see you too. Is Camden ready?"

My cue. I slowly walked through the den and living room to the front door. Dad and Cooper looked at me as I walked to the door. I felt good in my outfit. I had on the most beautiful purple Gloria Vanderbilt jeans with the perfect shade of lavender shirt with a peter pan rounded collar. The collar had a most delicate peeking of lace around it. Cooper told me how pretty I looked. Dad told us to have fun and to be home by 11:30 after the dance.

"Ok Dad."

I kissed Dad on the cheek, Cooper shook his hand and we hopped in the back seat. Michael and Susan both leaned back and said hello. We were off.

We left the dance a little early to go parking. Michael had bought some beer before picking us up. It wasn't hard to buy beer if you had a fake ID and June's minimart in town usually sold beer to some kids from our school as long as you had your ID.

Cooper and I each drank a beer. We made out in the backseat listening to R.E.O. Speed wagon "Keep on Loving You" until it was close to curfew and time to go home. We drove up to the front door and I took some mints to cover up the beer smell in my mouth. I kissed Cooper goodbye at the door one last time. Mom and Dad were in bed watching TV when I got home. I thought Mom had probably been drinking so it was easy not to have them smell the alcohol on my breath. I stood at their door.

"Did you have a good time at the dance?"

"I had so much fun, thank you for letting me go."

"Cooper is a nice boy. I like his parents," Dad said.

"Yes, he is. Good night."

Cooper and I were an item. We were always together in between classes and in the student lounge watching MTV. We would hold hands and sometimes I would sit in his lap until we got demerits for public display of affection, a PDA, from Mr. Summerbell.

At breaks and lunch, Mr. Summerbell would wander the halls looking for misdemeanors. He looked for reasons to give demerits to students. Demerits were handed out for no belt, PDA, yelling outside a classroom, rough housing, no socks, skipping class, and more. He was also a teacher when Dad was at school at Darlington. He had a square head with black slicked back hair, clean shaven face, wore angular flat top black rimmed glasses, and most everyday wore a dark suit, dark tie, and wingtip shoes. He dressed very formally and looked like he still taught in the 60's when Dad was in school. He looked uptight and never smiled while walking the halls. If someone saw him coming toward the student lounge, they would peek in and give a warning to all of us there so we could stop what we were doing and get in line before he walked through. It would get really quiet when he came in the lounge and it felt really awkward. Sometimes I felt sorry for him and that people made fun of him but he seemed to make it even worse on himself. I felt he could have been a little nicer and not so odd when he creeped around school.

At the end of the week, each person's demerits were counted up and posted where both day and dorm students could see it. For each demerit, we had to walk two laps around the lake, which sat in front of the drive at school and below the headmaster's home on the hill. Darlington School had been around since 1905 and had a beautiful main campus of woodlands and the lake around which most of the buildings are centered. The girl's dorm and the chapel were a little further away but still within walking distance from the lake. It was a beautiful focal point of the school with the leaves of the trees changing colors from greens to golds, yellows, reds, and oranges with the seasons and the two swans who lived in the lake year-round.

It was kind of cool to have demerits and walk the lake. The cool dorm students were out walking the lake. They had a lot more opportunity to get demerits because they were on campus 24/7 and could get demerits for not having their room clean at inspection, not having lights out, not being on campus by a certain time, not getting to church on Sundays, and more. I liked walking the lake and my eyes often wandered to some of the cute older dorm guys. I didn't want too many demerits though because I didn't want to spend my whole Friday after school there. I wanted to be with Cooper or get on with my weekend.

Cooper and I were the couple everyone thought would last forever and get married. We even talked around it some together but not directly to it at this point. We had been dating over a year. I was a sophomore now and he was a junior. He spent time at my house and I spent time at his a lot too watching TV, making out when our parents weren't around, listening to music and just hanging out. He went with me on summer vacation to Sea Island. He couldn't drive yet so Mom drove us in the Cadillac. It was as big as a boat, white outside and interior with a navy blue linen cloth top. Mom special ordered lots of gold bling. She liked it to be pretty. Rema, Cooper, and I sat in the backseat and Rema commented that she could live there it was so comfortable.

We were so bored on the way home, we did a makeover on Cooper and made him a girl. He had long eyelashes and the mascara we added gave him that extra feminine touch. A little blue eye shadow and some soft pink gloss completed his girly look. He actually looked quite pretty and what a great boyfriend for letting us make him over. I felt so lucky to call him my boyfriend. We had fun together. There was a simple quality to our love. It was young, fresh, and fun. We were exploring together.

My friends kept asking if we had 'done it' yet. "No, we haven't but we have done a lot." I knew he and I were both thinking about it. We hadn't talked about it but our making out was getting heated and it was getting harder to pull away from going further. We were both virgins. I knew what 'doing it' was but I didn't know how to do it and I didn't think he did either. Not long after my 15th birthday we talked about sex.

My friend Beth had done it. She said it wasn't so scary and she couldn't believe we hadn't done it yet. We had dated longer than she and David. Many thoughts were going on in my head. We should do it. We loved each other and we would get married one day so we should. I didn't want to get pregnant. I could have him pull out or we could use a condom. I wasn't on the pill. We talked about doing it and decided it was a good idea. We had been dating a long time and we did love each other.

We planned a date on Saturday night.

Cooper picked me up in his burnt orange ford Mustang coupe and we listened to 38 Special, "Hold on Loosely" while driving to the club. We went to the country club parking lot to meet our friends, hang out and have some beers. I had told my friend Beth that we were planning to do it, but just didn't know when. I had a feeling it would be this night, so I was ready. After hanging out a while and having a few beers, we decided to go to Cooper's house and watch TV. We drove up to his house in Maplewood, a sleepy family subdivision in Northeast Rome. We walked in the house and Jerry, Cooper's Dad was watching TV. Bess, his mom was just getting ready to go read in bed.

It was almost 10 and I didn't have to be home until 11:30. Cooper told his Dad we were going to watch TV in the backroom.

"Ok, just save enough time to get Camden home before 11:30. I don't want Frank mad."

He was right; you didn't want to see Dad mad or have him mad at you.

We went to the back of the house to Cooper's room to watch TV. We sat on the bed, turned on the TV and closed the door. I could hear the TV sound in the background. My attention was torn between kissing Cooper, his Dad in the room in the front of the house, the TV, and what I thought was about to happen. We were kissing and it started to go farther. Neither one of us knew what to do. We explored our way through each other's bodies, still mostly clothed.

He was on top of me. We fumbled our pants most of the way down. We both guided it inside me for what felt like only a few minutes, but still satisfactory and an accomplishment. He pulled out before he came because we wanted to be sure and be safe. I can't say it felt good or bad. It happened playfully and awkwardly, almost as if we felt we just had to get through this first practice time then we would know how to move forward.

Shit. A knock on the door and we were scrambling to tidy our clothes in place.

"Cooper, I think you need to get Camden home now. It's

close to her curfew time."

"Ok, Dad, thanks."

Strange, he didn't open the door to tell us. The light was out where we were but the TV was on so that wasn't unusual for us. He must have known what we were doing. I felt red rush to my face. He knew. How could I walk out the door and see him. He would know. I took a couple of extra minutes to get my clothes perfectly in place, my hair just right, and I took a couple of breaths and hugged Cooper. He looked just as guilty as I felt. I think I covered up my guilt better than he did. He was on the student council and was not a very good liar. I could pull it off. We walked past his Dad quicker than normal, doing our best not to make too much eye contact.

"Goodnight Mr. Crawford. Thank you for letting me come over and watch TV tonight."

"Goodnight Camden. Cooper, see you shortly?"

The next day Cooper called to talk. We talked about what we did but mainly we talked about his talk with his Dad when he got home. His Dad waited up for Cooper to come home after dropping me off. He asked Cooper to sit down, that he wanted to talk to him about me. He said he really liked me and that he knew Cooper loved me very much and that we loved each other. He also wanted us to be very careful because we were very young. He didn't want me to get pregnant and he said if we were having sex that we needed to make sure we were very careful. Cooper said he was so embarrassed and I could completely picture him sitting there with his Dad, face turning completely red.

We were very careful and made sure that he always pulled out before he came.

He was my first.

I told Beth.

I think most of my friends knew anyway. I felt like the whole school knew.

We had been dating over a year and it was time.

They're Back

The secret of change is to focus all of your energy not on fighting the old but on building the new.

Socrates

In 2004 we sold our Los Angeles

home in a week, packed up, and moved to Georgia for what Luke and I planned as an inquiry vacation to consider our next move. I had not lived in Georgia since I left for college when I was eighteen in 1984. I moved away to get away. I also moved away to see if I could hear myself.

Myself and not always the voices. Then I could see if the voices followed me. If they didn't follow me, they weren't mine. They were the sickness, the loneliness, and the void that I could leave behind forever and finally be happy.

What was happy? Happy was when everyone in our family got along together. Happy was when the voices would leave. Happy was when I felt loved and had the perfect life of marrying the man that would make all my dreams come true. We would have two children, a home where my husband came home from work each day happy to see me, and kissed me while looking into my eyes and meaning it when he said, "I love you."

Happy was when life was smooth and no one was angry. Happy was order in my life or so this was what I thought in my young mind.

I ran away to college when I was eighteen to be happy.

When we returned to Georgia in 2004 the voices came back. The bargaining with the voices. The bargaining with God. The bargaining with myself that if I could just exercise and lose weight, my body would be enough to keep the attention of my husband and he wouldn't find other women because I wasn't good enough.

If I drank too much one night, I would bargain with myself and God that I would never do it again if I would just feel better that moment and I wouldn't let it happen again. I wouldn't do to my children what I had experienced most of my life with my mother.

How could it possibly happen again when I vowed to not parent like my mother? When I vowed to be the best mom and be there for the girls?

I knew the impact my mother's drinking had on me when I was little and how it affected my relationships, my marriages, my self-esteem, my money, my worth, my value, and my love for myself. It was a slow suicide, for both of us. I did not love myself and I was dying in my heart a little bit each moment of every day.

I know I agreed with Luke that it would be a good move. I know he was excited to try living away from California since he never had before and at the same time I thought, *What the hell am I doing?*

The voices said "We can do this."

Then the voices changed their tune. I got back and it felt so strange in my body to be on this island where I had vacationed all of my life. I had some great memories there and I had some really old bitter and painful memories that resurfaced as the reminder of my failures at life. At first it was okay, I kept this sense about me of being in California.

The freedom to be who I was, the ability to live my life from my heart and not from the "shoulds" I knew all my life.

I knew this true freedom was inside me and yet, it began to get faint and the critical voices took control. I was smothered and imprisoned by my regrets, failures, and reminders that I wasn't good enough. Living in California was about freedom and finding myself and doing what I wanted to do. No one controlled me but I still had a secret; more than one.

My mother wasn't drinking anymore. She went to rehab and got sober in July 1986. But the secret was now my secret. It was a different secret. Actually it was the same secret and I was living with her pain still, my family's pain, and my own pain. I didn't deserve this life.

This secret, and others, were causing the same problems.

I didn't want anyone to know or they might not like me. They might even leave me and abandon me for good and then what would I do. I would be alone. They might laugh at me. They might call me stupid. I held it inside which I knew how to do. I knew how to stuff and manage my world so it worked out the way I wanted or so I thought.

I had a false sense of control in my life.

When things didn't work out the way I planned, I was thrown off course with brute force. I needed it to be perfect. I needed it to look nice on the outside even if it didn't feel so good on the inside and I knew it was messy. I could hide it and no one would see it or know.

Perfectionism was exhausting and drained me of every little bit of energy. Perfectionism was my way of saying that I was right and I am not wrong but what I thought and what the voices told me was that I was wrong most of the time. I was just plain wrong and so was everything about me. I was insecure about my looks and knew I didn't look like the women in Playboy. I wasn't smart enough. I didn't manage my money well.

I kept asking myself "Why in the hell are we living here?"

Independence Day, the first year we moved to Georgia. Our neighbors asked us over for a barbeque, or cookout, as we call it in the South. All of our kids were little and the fireworks were late so we thought it would be better to stay home, have some firecrackers and sparklers, and get them in bed early. I remember going next door, standing in the driveway and Luke looking at me and saying "You don't belong here. What have I done taking you away from California and back to Georgia."

I knew something felt off. I wanted to compromise and stay there for Luke. But I was feeling the claustrophobia of this island that was seventeen miles long and two miles wide.

We stayed and had dinner and it came time for fireworks. Our friends were outside, we had chairs in the driveway, and were ready to go.

Celebration.

It was familiar and like the old celebrations. There was alcohol and fighting. Our neighbors started fighting. It was a hushed fighting that I recognized from when I was little. It was glares. It was jabs with words. There were slurred words and walking away mad. So many experiences throwing me back to those hard memories that I went away from when I left at 18.

I could feel my body tense. I became a wall or fortress that wanted to ricochet any of those words or feelings that were trying to get inside me again. I just wanted to get them away. When there's a wall nothing can get in or out. So different than a boundary where there is respect and you can choose what gets in or out in a way that is healthy and clear. I couldn't get inside myself and yet I couldn't get outside myself either.

I was trapped.

Again.

Think of a wild animal that's trapped; what does it do? It snarls, it fights, it claws and it plays dead. When I was sober, I was quiet and good at playing dead if I was around someone who had hurt me. If I'd been drinking, I fought back. I reacted. I had to change something and usually that change was not healthy.

Drinking and walls do not mix.

They collide.

That's what happened on this island.

I had a collision with every memory that I wanted to block out and every new experience that brought up any of those memories. When there is a collision there is a crash and something or someone is hurt, damaged, or dies.

I was dying a little bit inside myself each day.

I was moving in extremes of living from good girl masking depression trying to hold everything in and play the role to the other extreme of being the party girl who likes to have fun and at the same time numbing so I don't feel the pain of being wrong. I was living a bipolar life.

I bargained to go out and just have one drink or just be good. It rarely happened and many times ended up embarrassing my husband.

One beautiful, sunny, Friday afternoon perfect beach day, we had planned an evening out with friends after a short photo shoot. During that week and at the shoot, I was feeling restless. I could feel the truth wanting to come up and out and I had to push harder to keep it down.

That night after the shoot we went to Rafters, a casual bar on the island, to hear a friend's band. It was smoky, people were everywhere, and I was in a mood and there was no stopping me.

She was out.

She was Lola.

Luke had given me this name not long after we met and he was introduced to my wild side. Lola was a pusher and Luke always said "Whatever Lola wants, Lola gets."

Did I really? Lola could be fun and then she wasn't. She could be scary too.

I think she has been my protector.

Here comes Lola…

I had some cocktails and we were dancing. I was feeling the truth wanting to come up and I knew I was combusting.

I couldn't take it anymore. The fakeness, the perfection, the pretending was killing me.

In the middle of the dance floor, dancing with my husband, around a packed room of a few friends and many strangers, I ripped off my bra and threw it to the band. That got some laughs from friends and a chuckle from Luke.

Knowing him though, I knew he was scared and nervous because he'd seen me in action before and it was something he didn't like at all. It scared him. After dancing more and another drink, it was time to go.

Luke handed me my bra and I took my shirt off in the middle of the dance floor around the crowd of people. I was standing in the middle of the crowd, shirtless and braless.

"What in the hell are you doing?" He yelled at me.

In that moment, I just needed it all to stop. Everything. Life was spinning out of control and I needed to act in that moment with control. What seemed like wild abandon and disrespect was a call for help from deep inside me to get me out of here, get me out of myself, and end this now.

I can't do this anymore.

I can't do this anymore.

Why am I here?

How do I make it stop?

I am not her. I am no one. I am so angry with myself.

I hate myself.

Braces

Though we travel the world over to find the beautiful, we must carry it with us or we find it not.

Ralph Waldo Emerson

The void can be so lonely. The void can talk to you. The void can be painful if you don't fill it with love for yourself first. This concept never entered my mind, my heart, my vocabulary. Nobody in my life spoke this language when I was growing up.

I was always hiding myself and so afraid to be me because I knew that no one would like me.

I wasn't pretty enough.

I was awkward.

I was not a pretty girl like Karen or Mary Kate and who would want to take me to a middle school dance. I stuffed all of these feelings down inside. I seemed confident on the outside, maybe a little shy, but I looked like I had things somewhat together. I covered up my unworthiness with my armor with the attitude of I'll win and show them. It was important for me to win at all costs.

I had full on, thick band, silver braces for 7th and 8th grade. They were tight, uncomfortable most of the time, and I could never eat a ham sandwich, which I loved on soft white Wonder Bread with mayo and mustard, without half of the bread getting stuck to the wires of my braces. It just hung on and wouldn't budge. My best bet was removal with a water pic or just don't eat the sandwich.

I opted out of ham sandwiches for two years.

I wore my night headgear one time and that was never happening again. Dr. Pridemore and his nurses pushed it on me each time I went for a checkup.

"The more you wear your headgear, the quicker you'll get these braces off and show off your gorgeous smile."

When they handed over the wire apparatus that looked like something for neck traction, they tried to make it fashionable.

"You can wear it at night and around the house during the day. It's got a quilted fashionable fabric neck padding for comfort and it looks great."

Really? Looks great on whom? The fabric did not make the idea of wearing this thing more palatable. The rebel in me silently spoke.

"I'm not wearing it."

I knew I wanted my braces off, so I did give it one try but only at night when no one would see me not even me because I was sleeping. I put it on, lied down the best I could on the pillow with wires wrapped around my jaw and connected to my teeth. I woke up in the middle of the night with a stabbing sensation in my neck. Shit. The metal ends had come out of my mouth, the headgear was mangled and the metal pieces were sticking in my neck. Not going to work.

Solution: lie on my checkups and tell them everything was great with the headgear and hope my teeth played along with my lie. Two years later, it worked.

Rema and I got our braces put on the same day and had them taken off the same day. We went to all of our checkups together. We had a couple of other friends join us too.

Braces were big and there was one orthodontist in Rome at the town. Dr. Pridemore was the best in town. He had a modern office with six chairs all arranged in one room; three on one side and three on the other. We were all able to go together and then after our appointments, the mom who took us to that checkup would take us to lunch.

We figured we could miss at least 2 or 3 hours of school doing it this way. It worked.

I remember the big day. Rema and I were giddy we were so happy to be done with braces. Dr. Pridemore told me I had done well with my headgear and I was getting them off in perfect timing. The lie worked. The headgear cooperated.

The hygienist pulled out dental pliers and began to snip the wires. There was a major construction zone in my mouth. My mouth was getting tired from staying open so long.

Drool pooling in my mouth. Suction tools drying out the drool. Crustiness surrounding my mouth and dry lips.

It's all worth it.

Pliers plucking the silver bands off each tooth one at a time. I was being freed. Liberated to live and join the ranks of high school freshmen coming into Darlington School. A rite of passage.

As the last band was popped from my tooth, I glanced over at all the metal on the dental tray hovering above my right shoulder.

Was it salvageable for sale?

It was junk but it was my junk that had given me a new look, new straight teeth and a new smile. A new face that people would see when they looked at me.

No more bugs bunny.

No more buck teeth that I had to cover by putting my hands near my face or trying to close my lips, which was not possible.

I closed my eyes again as she cleaned my teeth. I let me tongue take a sneak peek. I ran it across my upper teeth just for a quick preview. It was smooth and felt slimy. It had been a long time.

When she was done, she said, "You can see your teeth now."

"I don't want to see just yet. Let me feel them with my tongue."

I reached my tongue down to my bottom teeth and traced from right to left. Smooth as our new kitchen counter tops. A little slimy, almost like my spit didn't know where to go anymore since it didn't have the dam all built up.

My tongue jumped a level to my top teeth. I took it to the top two teeth and let it sit while I took in the feel of the straightness. No separation between the teeth, smooth and slimy too. I opened my eyes. I looked in the mirror and smiled.

I cried little tears inside for this big change on my outside.

I was pretty now.

No one would make fun of me.

I didn't have to cover up my mouth or feel like a baby anymore.

All outer evidence of sucking my thumb until 5th grade was gone. No one would know unless I told them, and I would never do that. Sucking thumbs was for babies and kids who were scared.

I was pretty now, but I wasn't the prettiest girl. Mary Kate and Karen were still the prettiest girls that all the boys liked.

I really didn't like any boys yet. I did kiss one boy in middle school but he just seemed to be eating my face. Disgusting. I didn't need that for sure. I did have a secret crush but I would never tell anyone. I knew he would never like me but it was fun when I felt he was flirting with me in French class. He said I had the prettiest legs.

Now I was pretty too.

Not the prettiest, but pretty.

I was pretty too.

Investigation

Yoga does not just change the way we see things, it transforms the person who sees.

B.K.S. Iyengar

When we moved back to Georgia, I
started drinking more.

I started smoking pot.

I was waking up after black-outs.

I was repeating the same pattern that my mother had when I was little.

Luke and I had our adorable, precious girls and I thought 'what am I doing?' I couldn't get out of the pattern, I was stuck, and I didn't know how to stop it.

How to stop it?

It was like I wanted to clean myself up on all levels. I wanted to let go of the bad tastes. Bad decisions a lifetime in the making.

I continued to suffocate the emotions inside me. It felt like I was holding a pillow over my own face, only allowing shallow sips of air to make it into my body. I was sustaining only the necessary parts of living. I replaced these emotions with staunch guardians of the gates: perfectionism, constant judgement of others, my critical voice, guilt, shame, people-pleasing, not worthy, selfish, not good enough, embarrassment, and dirty.

My voices.

I had heard Sabine was a gifted teacher and that she was tough. She would call you out. Her studio on St. Simons Island was "the yoga studio" for real yoga.

Sabine had a gift to be able to take you deep inside yourself when you were in class with her.

I discovered the feeling of being deep inside myself lasted even when I wasn't in class.

We had known each other for a while now and had also become friends. I still had a thread of alert around her. I wasn't always comfortable with her but I liked being with her. She was strong, opinionated, interesting in so many ways. She cooked exotic foods with spices I had never heard of with a combination of care and exciting flare.

I started to piece together all the parts of stories she told me about her life. She grew up in California. She had been shuffled around with care givers when she was a child. She had done drugs.

She was married to a Cuban man who lived in Miami, had two sons and grandchildren now.

She was an avid road biker.

She got hit by a car that messed up her body badly and yoga had given her so much wisdom and healing. She didn't seem to date but she did say she had before.

I was trying to piece it together all together and make sense of it.

Still observing. Still watching. Still trying to create meaning and ritual.

Her teachings seeped into all parts of my life. A simple question she would ask would keep me thinking and investigating my life for weeks. One day she asked me "Why do you drink?"

Sabine saw me. She got my attention. I thought she must

have seen an energy in me that gave her insight that this was just really the medicine that I needed. It was the lifeline that I needed that was going to give me a process.

When I started yoga I started to feel something.

I started to feel and see myself differently. I was reminded of my strength and began to bring it out of hiding.

I wondered if I could love myself.

When I started practicing yoga postures, I found this gave me a sense of being present in my body and clearing my mind of repeated critical scenarios. I felt liberated and open and the voices were quiet.

I started to really look at that for myself and I asked myself this really important question.

Would I say these things to a friend of mine? Would I actually say these things out loud that I am saying to myself inside my head? Would I say them to a friend of mine and how would they react?

I would never tell my friend, "You're not good enough; you're stupid, you don't do this well."

Why was saying that to myself?

Sabine told me, "You would be a great yoga instructor."

When I first started teaching, I thought, 'Oh my gosh; how am I going to do this?'

My perfectionism popped up. I thought I've got to be perfect and I wanted to hide all that wasn't. Not possible.

I stopped wearing my grandmother's ring. I thought you had to be poor to be a yoga instructor and give your life away to be in service.

I knew I shouldn't drink but I did and went over the edge more than once. There was a battle in me - drink, don't drink, bargain with God when I drank too much. I'll never do it again if I can just feel better tonight. Shoving the guilt and shame down inside.

Teaching yoga, drinking too much, trying to be a mom, needs to look perfect. How will I ever do all this? I can't do this. They're going to find out and then they won't like me. Why do I keep doing this? I want off this ride. I don't want to do this anymore.

Crash.

Hide.

Stuff.

Teach.

Love.

Try.

Sabine cultivated a yoga community. She had a strong policy for how things were done at the studio. As teachers, we were to arrive 30 minutes before our class. After class, we were to tidy the room, sweeping the yoga floor one aisle at a time to get all the dust away.

Arriving early gave us the opportunity to get the room prepared, any materials and teachings we needed to get ready and to energetically come to the space ourselves. This worked for me because I liked being on time and being early. It made me nervous whenever I thought I was going to be late to meet someone or to an event. I did my best to be on time or I was mostly always early.

As a teacher at the studio, I found myself wanting to please her, wanting to be right.

Falling Apart

It is by going down into the abyss that we recover the treasures of life. Where you stumble, there lies your treasure.

Joseph Campbell

They were married forty-three years.

I knew they were leading separate lives but I thought it would last.

It didn't.

Mom was devastated.

Dad was sad too.

On January 13, 2008 Dad left again. This time was the last time. My birthday.

A part of me was surprised. A part of me wasn't. A part of me was sad. A part of me got it. I didn't think either one of them was happy and that made me sad. I knew I couldn't do anything to help. They had to do what they needed to do.

I could tell as I watched them. I loved them both. I didn't want to pick sides. I didn't have to. I had to have

103

clear boundaries. How was that possible? I don't want to hurt anyone. I don't want anyone to be sad.

Can't we just be happy?

Why can't you talk and work it out?

Why can't you talk and move on with your separate lives and we can still be ok?

I felt ten years old again. It was happening for real this time. I felt in the middle. I felt responsible to help. I also had my family and was a wife and mother. It was a lot to juggle.

Stop.

I don't want to remember.

It's too much.

After our soccer game on Friday afternoon, we planned to head up to Athens to go to the University of Georgia football game. We were going to the big party at Chi Phi house on Friday night; we knew a lot of the guys because they had gone to our high school.

I can remember being in the locker room after the game. We were so excited: taking showers, getting ready. I loved my outfit of thin cords and a simple sweater.

I was a junior in high school and seventeen and I had a lot of friends who were seniors and in college. I had lots of friends.

It was about a two hour drive from Rome to Athens. We had a couple of beers on the way there and some food. We arrived at the Chi Phi house and the party was roaring. Lots of music, drinks, and people. It was time to catch up to the others. We drank some more and saw some friends from school.

I ran into one of my friend's boyfriend. He came alone that weekend and she stayed home. We started chatting and then went upstairs to get high in his friend's room in the fraternity house.

It happened so quickly.

I didn't see it coming.

He pushed my body down on the bed and held my shoulders and started kissing me. He then put his hand over my mouth so hard I couldn't move.

I froze and was paralyzed.

He told me to be quiet.

He took his hand off my mouth and pulled my pants to my ankles. One of his hands returned to my mouth and the other on my hip. I didn't move. The tears were hot and salty as they ran down my face. He finished and told me to get dressed. He went downstairs.

I wiped my eyes, pulled my pants up, and went back downstairs.

I pretended it didn't happen.

I stuffed feelings of guilt, shame, embarrassment because it must have been my fault somehow. There was no way I could tell anyone because they would think I was bad and that it was me. I should have been a good girl and it never would have happened.

Mom would say, *If you lay down with dogs you get up with fleas.*

One day, while living in the house on Collinwood Road, Mom had been drinking most of the day. She was on her usual routine of drinking vodka and orange juice toward the morning and then had switched to Ernest Gallo white wine (the big see through green bottle jug on the top shelf of the refrigerator).

It was a Saturday and Dad was playing golf.

Brother and I were playing at the house.

It was late afternoon early evening time and Dad wasn't home yet. Mom was talking on the phone slurring her words and seemed to be drunker than normal for this time of day.

Watch carefully.

I was already "the little mom".

It was important to see what was happening so I could make sure we were safe and I could respond however I needed to keep us that way. I was watching mom from the dining room and listening without her knowing. She got off the phone and starting walking to the bathroom. I could hear her talking under her breath and I could hear her stumbling.

I walked parallel to her on the other side of the house so I could make sure she didn't fall, or if she did that I was there to help her. She made it to her bathroom and I was peeking around the corner at her.

She saw me and told me to come out.

I did and she was sitting on the toilet wobbling side to side. Her face was weird and distorted looking and she was mad.

She asked what I was doing.

I told her I just wanted to make sure she made it to the bathroom okay. That made her madder.

She looked at me in the eyes with as much focus as her eyes would make and she said, "I hate you."

She flipped me off.

"I hate you."

It hit me like an arrow that blew up in my heart. I felt sick to my stomach. Then she said, "You are so selfish."

I was thirty years old and felt it was time. There was never any agreement about when I was supposed to be able to use it. Mom took care of it herself; she and Nannie always reminded me, "Don't ever give your money away, keep it separate from your husband, and don't be foolish because you can never make it back."

I asked if I could have my money. I could take care of it and manage it.

Mom said, "No, you won't do it right. I don't think you're ready. I'm going to continue to take care of it. Nannie and I worked hard to save it for you and I don't want you to spend it all because you'll never be able to make it back."

I felt two years old again. I thought I was responsible,

organized and ready but the old voices started up in my head.

Was she right?

Dad is an attorney. He talked to me privately because he believed I was ready to take care of my money. He said, "We can sue your mother for that money because it's rightfully yours. It became yours when you were 18; is this something that you want to do? We won't go to court but it will motivate her to give you what is yours."

I trusted Dad's advice and agreed. I had always walked a tightrope or ridden the middle line of the road with my parents. From what I saw, I understood why each reacted the way they did to each other. I understood Dad's anger when Mom would drink and I understood Mom's sadness when Dad did not give her attention.

We presented Mom with the papers. She stood up, looked at me, started crying and left the room. I walked outside and was standing by the horse paddock talking to Dad. Mom came outside and said she would sign the papers and I could have my money. She was shaking and crying and mad.

"You are both the most selfish people I have ever known in my life. No one has ever treated me like this. You are ungrateful and you should be more thankful that your Nannie and I did this for you."

She signed the papers and left them in my room.

She wouldn't talk to me. I packed my things and told them I was leaving early for California. There was no sense staying if no one was going to talk.

Cooper and I were not doing well and it was mostly my doing. I was pushing him away. I had it in my mind that I needed to see other people. He would be leaving for school in a year and maybe it was better if we broke up now.

I was scared of him leaving me.

I didn't want to be alone but if I broke up with him now, I could date and find someone else and I wouldn't be alone.

I was confused. The voices were driving me crazy.

I broke up with him. He was upset. I was upset.

Weeks passed.

His friends were mad and mean to me. I ran away by drinking and partying. I stayed away from him and then I wanted him back but he was seeing someone already. He said he had a date with her and liked her. She was nice.

I stopped eating. I thought if I got thinner he would pay attention to me again. I could feel my hip bones and collar bones sticking out and I liked it. I was so thin. I liked it when people said how thin I was because I had been trying to have thin thighs for so long.

I felt tired, weak and sad.

A distraction came soon. A dorm student, Jeff asked me out. He was going home to Atlanta for the weekend. He asked me to drive down on Saturday spend the day, have lunch, and hang out. He was cute in a rebel bad boy way.

He had dated my cousin's best friend, Jenny, when I was about twelve. I saw Jeff then too but I don't think he remembered me buck teeth and awkward. Jenny was so beautiful. Tall, thin, gorgeous skin, and beautiful long hair.

I couldn't believe he was asking me out.

I knew my parents wouldn't let me go. I lied to them and told them I was going out for the day and would be home in the afternoon. I drove to Jeff's Mom's condo in Atlanta. He greeted me at the door and gave me a kiss. I was shy and looked away.

He asked me in and offered me a beer.

That's what I needed. It would calm me down and pep me up. He showed me around their home. His mom was gone and we were alone. As we walked through the house, he kissed me long and slow in the doorways in between the rooms. I almost fell to my knees.

Was this really happening?

He was one of the cutest seniors and he was a dorm student, which made it even more daring. He showed me a bathroom where I could change into my bathing suit. We were going to hang out at the pool after we ate.

I changed into my string bikini which I could wear now that I was so thin. I pulled my shirt and shorts over it. We continued walking through the house. He took me into his room and asked if I wanted to see his gun.

See his gun?

He took the shoe box from the top closet shelf and took off the top. He pulled out the revolver and told me his Dad killed himself with this gun.

Was he going to hurt me?

What had I gotten myself into by coming here?

I must have seen the look on my face because he put the gun away and the box back on the top shelf. He asked if I was hungry or wanted to get high first. I was ready to get high. I hadn't really smoked pot yet, maybe just a puff or two, but right now, I wanted anything to move on from where we had been.

He pulled out a joint, lit it, and took a puff.

My turn.

A long puff and a lot of coughing.

Between the beer and the pot, I was feeling spacey. I was out of it. We stood in the kitchen, making out. I was half feeling my body and half thinking it felt like it belonged to someone else.

I needed to eat.

I needed food or I was going to fall down. We got some food from the fridge which he had ready for us and took it by the pool.

I took off my shirt and shorts and he told me how sexy I was. No one had ever said those words to me before. I was sexy like the girls in Playboy, like Jenny too. Me, sexy?

He stroked his fingers along my stomach.

We ate.

We swam.

I went inside to get another beer. He followed me. We had sex in his room on the bed. The kisses were slow and the sex was fast.

I couldn't believe I had sex with him. He had sex with me.

Maybe being without Cooper wasn't so bad.

I could do this.

I would be okay.

I would be okay.

I had to drive home soon. I was already going to be late and had to tell my parents something. I would figure that out on the hour drive home. Some more food and a swim should help. Then I kissed him and said goodbye.

On the drive home, it started to get dark. It was way later than I had told my parents. I told them I would be home in the early afternoon, even though that had never been my plan.

It was already the evening and I was still driving.

The voices started up:

I shouldn't have smoked pot.

I should have eaten more.

I shouldn't have had sex with him.

I was coming down hard. I didn't want to go home and tell my parents another excuse. I pulled into the Ramada Inn parking lot, left the car on, lay down in the front seat and went to sleep.

Maybe I wouldn't wake up.

That would make it easier.

No excuses.

No more pain.

I could let go.

I woke up and it was dark. Shit. Eight o'clock. I put the car in drive and started home. I would tell my parents something, I just wasn't sure what. We were running late. We decided to swim longer and I forgot to call. I'm so sorry. That's it. It wouldn't matter anyway.

Nothing really mattered.

A few months went by and things had calmed down a bit. Kolton seemed to be better. I was living with friends, in a great apartment close to campus. We were dating, but not together all the time.

I had forgotten to take my birth control pill for a few days this month but was back to daily dosages. We were sleeping together regularly whenever I saw him. I noticed my breasts were swollen and killing me and I was late.

I went to a drug store way off campus and bought a few different pregnancy tests. They were positive and I was pregnant.

I was pregnant.

I didn't have a doctor at LSU. I talked to my roommates about what to do. I did not think having this baby was an option or a good idea.

I was pregnant.

It was surreal. Except that if I was being honest with myself, I did this on purpose. I quickly pushed down the reality of what I had done. I wanted to know what it felt like to be pregnant and I wanted to see if it would change him.

If it would change us.

Still, it wasn't real to me. How could this happen? I didn't even really think I could get pregnant.

I decided to have an abortion and told Kolton I had already made my choice. He told me he would get the money from his brother. I found out many years later he got the money from a friend and he spent the money from his brother on drugs.

My roommates and I picked out a clinic in Baton Rouge. I called the clinic and made an appointment. I was over 18 so I didn't need my parent's permission. They cautioned me there may be people picketing out front when I arrived but that it was my right and choice to make this decision if that's what I wanted.

I drove myself to the clinic. They were very comforting. I was nervous. I was so young and remember feeling so adult.

They told me everything I needed to know about the procedure and how to take care of myself after. They had me change and wait on a cot; there were other women waiting their turn. The nurse was very caring who came to get me. I went in to see the doctor and they gave me a shot inside my vagina and started the procedure.

Did it really happen?

Yes.

Tears running down my face.

Chest tight, heart racing.

Paralyzed.

The voices in my head:

I did it again.

Why was I so stupid?

I felt groggy getting up from the table. The nurse helped me up, gave me a giant pad to put in my panties to soak the blood from the abortion. She kindly took my arm and led me to the cot to lie down and rest before going home. I closed my eyes and tried to still my mind.

She offered me some apple juice and saltine crackers and just like when I was little it made it all better for now. She told me what to take for cramping and said there would be bleeding like my period but if it was unusually heavy to go to the emergency room.

My belly was crampy in knots and spasms as I drove myself back to the apartment. Kolton came over that night to check on me and took me to dinner. After dinner I came home and went to bed.

I never told my parents.

I hit rock bottom when the children were young. I was sitting in my closet, I was sick, I was crying, and I was trying to figure out how to kill myself so that my husband would get the life insurance money and be able to take care of the girls.

I remember thinking, *this isn't rational.* I remember thinking it was an option; it was definitely an option for me.

Death was always an option for me because it gave me an out and made it easier for other people around me, and I could make it better for people; I wouldn't be a burden anymore.

Death was an option.

I wouldn't hurt people.

I wouldn't be a burden anymore.

I owed money to the IRS because I had cashed in most of my stocks in my trust. I didn't have any money left. I hadn't told anyone, not even Luke.

I had to tell him.

I had to tell Dad.

The voices came back.

I couldn't tell anyone.

What would they think?

They wouldn't understand.

I was stupid to spend my money.

I was selfish just like Mom said and I couldn't manage money.

It was my fault and I had to make it right.

I was desperately thinking of ways to make more money. I was working and making good money with private clients and yoga but that wasn't enough for what I owed the IRS. I would never catch up. I needed money and I needed it now. I remembered someone mentioned amateur night at the strip club off highway 95 and that we should go just for fun. They were joking, but I secretly considered it.

What if I went to the bunny ranch in Nevada for a week, could I do that and make the money I needed?

I was frantic, irrational and scared. My family would be better off without me.

I'm a dead weight.

I'm sick.

I'm tired all the time.

I hold Luke back and don't want to socialize and go out much.

I'm not patient with the girls after a night of drinking and I'm a horrible mom for getting drunk and being hungover.

Why am I drinking like Mom?

Didn't I learn anything and why do I keep doing it.

These secrets are killing me.

I don't want to be here anymore.

Does my insurance coverage cover suicide?

How could I kill myself and Luke would still get the insurance money?

I needed the voices to stop. I needed it all to stop. I needed a way out. I could have a car accident but if there weren't skid marks to stop they could prove it was suicide. Are there pills I can take that wouldn't be detected? The thoughts in my mind continued to swarm. I was sobbing on the floor of my closet with the door closed.

The first time was when I was sixteen.

I can see myself on that summer night. I went out in my bright, shocking pink and yellow, strapless, Lily Pulitzer sundress. I was perfectly tan.

I had been driving since my birthday in January and I was feeling invincible, adult, and capable of managing my life. I had the best car ever, black Buick regal, tan interior, Blaupunkt stereo and t-tops. The exact car I wanted and the keys were wrapped and in a box for me from my parents for Christmas although my birthday wasn't until January.

That summer, I felt the independence and freedom my car gave me. I was driving everywhere with my friends and so loved it.

One July night, I was invited to a pool party with some friends and some older guys who had already graduated from high school. This was my playground. The older guys were intriguing and it got me attention from them and my friends for hanging out with the good looking, "bad boy" types. We went to the mini market and bought beer to take to the party and we knew they would have some other things too.

At this age, it was mostly pot, beer, and liquor. We got to the party and there were just about ten of us hanging out in the pool. I started drinking before we got there. I drank fast; I was on a mission to get drunk or high.

Mission accomplished and I was feeling no pain.

He was flirting with me and I liked it. He was older, in college, and cute. He was paying attention to me. It felt good to have him say nice things to me and think I was pretty. He grabbed my hand and walked me to my car.

Things were getting fuzzier. I was drunk and high trying to keep it together. I stumbled to the car. I wanted to lie down and go to sleep for a little bit. I couldn't talk because the words weren't formulated from my head to my mouth. They were stuck in the fog of numbness.

He guided me to the front seat, opened the door, placed me down along the front seat with my head toward the steering wheel and my legs dangling over the passenger side of the seat, out the door. My feet weren't touching the ground and the passenger door was open. I was hanging half out of my car.

It was dark on the street and I had parked in the trees so no one was around.

I felt like I was floating.

The t-tops of my car were open and I could see the tree branches swaying in front of the backdrop of a midnight blue black dark sky.

For a moment I was distracted by this wonder and beauty of what was above me and then I felt my dress being pushed up above my waist. I couldn't move and I couldn't speak.

I wasn't a virgin.

I wasn't a prude.

I laid there.

I couldn't move or speak.

He smelled like beer and his scruff on his beard scratched on my face as he moved up and down on top of me. He was heavy and then I didn't feel him at all. I couldn't move and I couldn't speak. I was floating. I kept my gaze on the tree branches in the sky and I kept them there strong and steady. I let it happen. He finished and got up off of my body. He said he would walk back up to the party first. Then told me I could come back to the party.

He went back.

I got up and stumbled back up to the party, found the bathroom, washed my face, and went back out to the party. I pulled it together, got everyone who was riding with me.

I went home and went to bed.

The next morning I went outside to make sure my car was parked straight in the driveway, there were no beer bottles in the car or any evidence of the night before. I didn't want my parents to know anything. I didn't want to remember anything.

I brought this on myself and it was my fault.

The voices said "If you were just a good girl this never would have happened." I believed them.

I would never mention this to anyone and if I stuffed it down far enough maybe I could forget it too.

Another Land

Adventure isn't hanging on a rope off the side of a mountain. Adventure is an attitude that we must apply to the day to day obstacles of life.

John Amatt

I was a picky eater and the peanut

butter was gone.

Eating was a not my priority and if anything I avoided it. I still kept an observant eye out for something I could eat, but my focus was elsewhere. One night there was a family dinner at the flat in Cairo. All of their relatives and many friends came. So much talking and so many people to say hello to. So much food prepared and on the table. None of it looked familiar but the white rice.

I could eat white rice!

It was now time to eat.

I took my plate from the buffet in the dining room and started walking around the table, serving myself very small portions of the food so I wouldn't be rude. I took the rice spoon, my mouth was watering since I hadn't eaten much in days, and I filled half my plate with white rice. I couldn't wait to dig in.

Then one of Rema's many aunts spooned a thick green liquid with okra on my rice.

"This is how we eat it," she said.

It was called Bamya, an okra stew. This okra was not fried like Mom's. My knees buckled underneath my wispy body and I almost fell to the ground.

How could I eat this rice now?

How could I get another plate without hurting anyone's feelings?

I would just need to sit down, try to eat something and just push the rest around to make it look eaten.

Driving was an experience in Egypt. Being a passenger in the car, I got to see everything. There were cars everywhere, people, sometimes animals, buildings and a completely different view than I had ever seen.

One day, we had a small wreck in traffic. People were yelling at us to move. Rema's grandfather was yelling back. We all got out of the car and started to push, while Rema's grandfather steered the car. Even her aunt got out to push; Rema and I had to laugh because she was only putting one finger on the car to push.

How was this helping? She was double our size and would sure lend lots of strength to the push with more effort.

Going to the Giza Pyramids was like being in a movie. Rema, Rema's little brother, Ron, and I got on our camels and were led out to the Sphinx. I was wearing my favorite t-shirt, maroon with a decal photo of Andy Gibb on the front, which I had made at the mall t-shirt store before I left. Ron's camel was spitting everywhere and tried to lie down with him on the camel's back. Rema and I couldn't stop laughing.

The guides led our camels and us to the sphinx. As we got closer, it got bigger and bigger. Then we got off our camels and ran quickly over to the pyramids and we started to climb one. We wanted to get off the sand as quickly as we could. It was so hot. We were able to climb the first few levels and then the stones were so large we couldn't make it up. The stones were strong and not moving at all. They had a red, orange brown tint to them. I kept wondering how they could have moved these stones and built these humongous pyramids with no cranes or equipment. I felt powerful and small at the same time. How did they do this?

I wondered what was inside and were there mummies and treasure that hadn't been found yet.

During our trip, one of Rema's cousins was getting married and we were invited. It was a beautiful wedding. The groom was handsome in his tux and the bride was beautiful in her traditional gown. It was a celebration and big lavish reception. Belly dancing is a key part of Egyptian wedding ceremonies and is used to celebrate joy and fertility. Families often have their marriage blessed by a performance from a belly dancer as part of the wedding celebration. There were dozens of belly dancers at the celebration wearing bright-colored traditional outfits with elaborate jewelry. They danced for us as a ceremony and they danced on our tables where we sat too.

They had sexy, shapely bodies with large breasts and big friendly smiles on their beautiful faces. Rema and I loved watching them. We went to the bathroom as they were performing and got to see them freshening their makeup and wiping the sweat so they could return to the lively festivities. I was envious of their breasts and how beautiful they were. It reminded me of the Playboy magazines Dad had on his nightstand and that my babysitters would look at when they came over.

Would I ever be that beautiful and desired?

Back to the party, it was fun to watch everyone dancing, drinking, smoking, and being so happy. The night went late and we fought being tired. We didn't want to say goodbye and miss anything. Beauty and love was everywhere and I felt it and wanted to hold on to it. I wanted to remember this night always and bring it back to me when I needed it at home.

We packed up the small station wagon with our bags, snacks, and family. We were ready for the drive through the desert from Cairo to Alexandria. It was around a three hour drive depending on our speed, how often we stopped and what we might see.

Rema's grandmother, Lulu, was bringing her dog, Jet. Jet was going with us for the trip. Jet was a black standard poodle, smart enough to acknowledge to us that he was always getting preferential treatment. Jet was her third child after her daughters, Mrs. Mixon, and her sister, Mervette. Jet was top dog and he knew it and milked it for everything he could. Jet wasn't really a dog that played with us but he did love Lulu. I admired his loyalty and devotion to her happiness.

We loaded in the car and were quite squished. Jet had the best seat and the most room in the car. How did that happen? I was used to animals because we always had more than one dog and cat growing up. I loved them but this was pushing my limits. Plus the fact that I had barely eaten in two weeks and was feeling weak and my stomach was constantly cramping and hungry.

At twelve, I was at the gawky stage of growth somewhere between a Great Dane puppy not knowing where it's limbs are and pouncing all over the place and a cat who's just been given a bath and feels completely vulnerable and exposed. I thought everyone noticed my buck teeth, gawkiness, budding breasts, and big feet. Here, I felt even more self-conscious of how I looked and how I acted and spoke. Jet was not helping things at all.

Ok, all loaded and ready. The windows were down because the air conditioner wasn't pumping enough cool air as we drove. If it got too windy or a sand storm blew up, we would close the windows, but for now, they were open and it was hot. I said a prayer and asked that we not break down in the car and that we make it safely. Just for good measure, I said a few Hail Mary's. It didn't matter that I wasn't Catholic. I think it still works the same.

We made it to the Petro station, the only building within miles of desert, sand, and road. They had gas, Fanta's, and snacks. We got an orange Fanta and it quenched my thirst and filled my tummy for now. Once in the car and on the road, Lulu asked, "Would you like to taste a prickly pear, Camden?"

"No thank you."

"Oh, come on, you'll love it once you bite in, don't mind what it looks like now."

It looked intimidating to me and not appetizing to my taste buds at all. She cut off the top layer and gave me a slice insisting that I eat a small bit. I gave in and did it. I can't say I much like it or disliked it. I was still stuck on the fact that she made me eat it. Just like my parents make me eat things I don't want.

I didn't want it.

Doesn't anyone listen to me?

As we got ready to pull away from the Petro station, we saw a group of people walking from the dessert to the station. They were covered head to toe in all black, even their faces; the only parts that were visibly human were their eyes and hands. Mrs. Mixon said they were Bedouins and they often wandered the desert. She said their name meant "desert dwellers" in Arabic and they were considered a nomadic tribe.

I asked if they were like gypsies. I had only seen gypsies in movies or read about them in books. This was so cool to see them and I felt like I was in a distant faraway land where anything was possible. I reminded myself to keep my eyes open so I don't miss a thing.

The high rise apartment in Alexandria was smaller than the flat in Cairo but it was stylish, modern, and decorated in white. White shag rug, white couch, and a sliding glass door to the deck that overlooked the multiple houses, apartments, and buildings in the city.

I loved it.

I always wanted to live in a city where no one knew you

except those you wanted to know. You could move in and out of life with sophistication, purpose, and independence in a city. We would sleep here at night and spend our days at the beach club cabana where we would swim in the sea.

This was cool. This was it. I had dreamed about this. It seemed familiar in ways that touched feelings I had dreamt about. We were going to meet some more of Rema's cousins, Cookie and Saraya. They were a little closer to our age. I thought maybe we would play with them at the beach.

I knew the beach. I knew the water. I felt at home with them both. We landed at our home for the day at the beach club. The sea was gorgeous. There were a lot more rocks at this beach than at Sea Island or Anna Maria Island, but water was water. While Mrs. Mixon put our food away for the day and arranged our bags, we went behind the curtain in the main room and changed into our suits.

I loved my new suit. It was a white off-one-shoulder one piece with red piping. It was flattering and functional. I could sunbathe, which Rema and I loved doing, and I could body surf. Before coming to Alexandria, Mr. Farid and Mrs. Mixon warned us of the very hot temperatures and that at all times, except in the water, we must keep our heads covered or we could overheat and get heat stroke. Rema and I were kind of professional when it came to lying out in the sun. We had dark skin and tanned easily. I used Tropicana or Hawaiian Tropic SPF 2 and Rema loved Coppertone SPF 4.

We timed ourselves when in the sun, thirty minutes on the front and then flip, thirty minutes on the back. It was super-hot here and I thought we might need to switch that to fifteen minutes and flip, then a swim. To cover our heads, Mrs. Mixon helped put the tall, free-standing umbrella in the sand and we lay down on the straw blanket with just our head covered by the shade of the umbrella. That way our bodies would get plenty of sun.

That day the waves were crazy; big and strong for body surfing. There was a pole with a flag that let us know if the current was okay for swimming; if it was black, we weren't supposed to go in the water that day. It was yellow that day and we ran to the water. All of us started body surfing. Swimming out, waiting for the perfect wave, paddling, kicking, and catching the wave, flying with our arms out like Superman. When the wave crashed, it crashed on top of me and it felt like I was under for minutes at a time, tumbling with the sand and tiny rocks. I tried hard to swim to the surface but the waves kept me below. Finally, I bobbed up with the foam of the after wave and gasped for an in breath.

We lost Ron. He was still under the waves. The lifeguard on the beach jumped in the water and disappeared. Next thing we saw was Mrs. Mixon running to the beach and the lifeguard pulling Ron to the shore. He was breathing but crying and scared. We almost lost him for good.

Kids bounce back fast. Adults not so much. Mrs. Mixon took Ron to rest in the cabana while Rema and I had some snacks. While I went in to use the bathroom, I peeked in on Cookie and Saraya as they were performing Salat, their Muslim prayers.

Rema was not Muslim. They were Episcopalian. Her grandfather was Muslim. Her grandmother was not. The prayers fascinated me. The movements. The dedication and focus of those saying and doing the prayers. A ritual like saying the rosary and going to mass that I had experienced at St. Mary's. I was still curious. Those who prayed at mass or doing the Salat seemed so at peace doing it and right after. It connected them to something that seemed to give them peace and a belonging.

I wanted to belong.

While visiting Alexandria, we went to go visit another aunt, Auntie Futma. She was quite large and was sitting on a tall bed in her apartment when we met her. When we arrived, she seemed to be praying or just finishing as there was incense burning and she was peaceful too. She grabbed me to hug me and kiss me and was so happy to see us. We visited for a while with her and this part of the family and then returned to the white apartment.

We woke in the early morning to a horrid smell. Rema and I had slept on the couch in the main room. Mrs. Mixon turned on the lights and Ron had gotten sick with diarrhea all over the white shag rug. The smell made us gag and Rema was sounding off with gagging noises making fun of Ron. Mrs. Mixon called the doctor to come see Ron and asked him to take a look at me too since I had lost so much weight by not eating much in almost three weeks.

Ron had some sort of bug or worm and was taking medicine to get better. I would be fine, but did need to eat some to get my strength back. It wouldn't be too long before we would fly home. I hadn't talked to my parents the whole trip. We weren't able to get through on the phone. I wondered what life had been like here when Mrs. Mixon was a little girl.

What would it be like for me to grow up here?

We flew home and slept most of the way. My parents came to the airport to pick me up. Mom was crying when she saw me. I was happy to see them and sad to say goodbye to my adopted family. She sat in the back seat with me while Dad drove.

She insisted we go through the McDonald's drive thru and order several cheeseburgers. I ate one. She made me eat another. I was too full and feeling smothered in the backseat.

I let her hold me and fell asleep on the ride home.

Change

Only in the darkness can you see the stars.

Martin Luther King Jr.

I took my first yoga class when I

moved to California. It was a Bikram class on Caledonia Street in Sausalito. The room was a tiny, vertically-challenged room, not big at all, with mirrors in the front, thick carpet on the floor, and two windows on the opposite wall.

The instructor was toned and well-built. He checked us in for class while sporting his navy blue speedo. And nothing else. Speedos were for swim team I remembered from growing up.

"We don't wear those at the country club" Mom told Brother when he was eight. This was not proper. Boys and men wore more traditional, southern, preppy swim trunks that came mid-thigh or just above the knee; mostly solid colors but sometimes speckled with a preppy pattern such as pink whales, lobsters, or a simple geometric splash. Certainly not a speedo.

As people checked in, they picked their spot, and started warming up with simple moves while taking short glances in the mirror. I did some of my stretches I knew from personal training and I felt proficient for the time being. The studio door closed, the heater started warming the room, and the yogis stood still in their speedos or skimpy workout clothes. I had "new girl" written all over me.

I'm okay, I thought, I can do this.

The poses were doable, the style of breath was new to me. The heat was intense at 105 degrees, even more concentrated and thick than an August day at home in Georgia. The room was small, the smell took over; the mirror and my determination kept me going.

It was grueling.

I was soaking wet.

I easily fell into the final pose of lying down on my back on the thick, sweaty, smelly carpet and it was heaven. My thoughts were distant. They didn't have a hold on me.

While I liked the Bikram, especially on a cold foggy day in Sausalito, I wanted to try some different classes. Yoga of Sausalito offered several different styles of yoga. Completely different than the Bikram yoga classes I had done, but same in the end result: my mind seemed calmer. There was space. I liked it. I felt a new understanding of what peace is to me. The quiet, uncollected me.

I wasn't planning.

I wasn't controlling.

I didn't have to be "on".

I was learning to let go and surrender.

I remember hearing many times yoga is a practice, letting go is a practice, surrender is a practice. A practice meaning that we discipline ourselves and commit to do it over and over until we become more proficient and masterful at this dedicated practice. I was just starting to take baby steps. I wasn't committed yet, but I liked how I felt after a yoga class.

I was also still hooked to the fast-forward feeling my workouts gave me. I loved hill sprints, lifting weights, kickboxing, aerobics, step, and boot camp workouts. I loved to push and keep pushing.

This was in my workouts and still in my life.

I was still pushing to get what I wanted and what I thought I needed to be happy. Again, I found myself riding the tightrope of two different lives. Inside I still felt I needed to prove I was worthy and good enough. I was unconsciously enmeshed in my same pattern of spending money on material things to prove my value and acceptance and help me feel better. It was a temporary fix.

I had nightmares about Kolton and that we were in love and together and then he would turn on me and hurt me. I would be crying in my sleep and Luke would wake me and ask if I was okay.

It messed with my mind. Why was this still coming up? I didn't want to be alone. Would Luke ever leave me?

The voices were still speaking and I did my best to quiet them with shopping sprees, workouts, drinking, an occasional high, and anything that would shut them up. That's what I knew worked.

But now yoga was showing me another way.

Which way to go?

I started hiking out to Tennessee Valley, climbing the stairs to a perch overlooking the Pacific Ocean. I talked to God. I forgave myself. I cried and screamed.

Was there more?

I had so much to purge, so much to let go of and it seemed to keep coming.

Would there be an end?

Would I ever just get there and be happy?

Yoga put me in touch with God within me in a way that I had never felt this presence or beingness before. God was not a man. God was a presence, a beingness within all things. This presence felt powerful, expansive, humbling, and nurturing.

I think this is what home feels like.

My yoga practice shifted while I was pregnant in 2001 and 2002. I was taking prenatal classes twice a week with kind, warm, and knowledgeable teachers. We moved through gentle flows and sequences, breathing slowly and attentively to our growing bodies and babies. We attuned to our needs as we softened our resistance to the changes in every part of our life.

During my first pregnancy, with Lily, I was still personal training with private clients up until I was seven months pregnant. I was also still working out but the prenatal yoga was offering me a rhythm I recognized had been missing in my life. I started to slow down. I felt a new found freedom in my body to be with the experience of pregnancy. I was in my own bubble and did my best to include Luke in my changes.

He was in his own bubble and his own changes. I wasn't drinking or wanting to go to parties or bars so much. It was overstimulating and not so much fun to be around people who were getting drunk. Something was out of sync about it for me.

Luke was drinking often and too much. He was having a hard time handling the change. I know he was excited. He told me so, but it was a big responsibility and would change our lives forever he said.

I loved him and was blown away that we had created this little baby in my belly. The miracle was evident to me and becoming more evident to him as he felt the kicks and flutters with his hand on my belly. I wanted to include him in as much as I could.

One night he came home to our little apartment and I'd never seen him so drunk.

Something had to change.

I talked to him the next morning. He agreed and admitted he was so nervous and was having a hard time with the change. It was real and unreal to him because his body wasn't changing but everything in his life was. We decided to go to the bookstore, movies, walks, and have dates that didn't involve drinking. That would make it much easier and sync up our shifts more closely.

I was in labor so long with Lily I lost sight and recognition of what I was doing. In the hospital there were no clocks on the wall or no watch on my wrist. I was in a time tunnel where the only time that existed was the waiting time of the labor and her birth. It was taking so long and my contractions had disappeared when the epidural was given to me. It was seventy hours before we met our first baby girl when she was delivered to us by C-section.

She was perfectly cone headed and crying when they placed her near me. They whisked her away to be cleaned, weighed and measured. Luke went with her as they shoved my organs back into my body and sewed me up. Thank God my doula, Bonnie, was with me. It was a very strange experience.

On the one hand euphoria greeting our new baby girl. On the other hand, such a rough experience with the labor and C-section. It was all worth it of course but this new life for all of us was going to take lots of love, commitment and acceptance of change.

It would take some time before I was working out and going to yoga again.

When Lily was five months old, I got pregnant. Since I had a miscarriage before Lily, and I was thirty-six years old, we decided to let whatever happen that was meant to happen. We used no birth control. I was also visiting my acupuncturist weekly to help my hormones and body recover from my pregnancy and birth of Lily.

My acupuncturist suggested I wait to get pregnant again so my body could recover more but I didn't want to because I was nervous I wouldn't be able to have another child. Right away I had nausea but no throwing up. I had acupressure to help with the nausea and ate lots of ginger biscuits from Whole Foods bakery. I heard ginger helped with nausea so I also had ginger lollipops.

This pregnancy felt different. I was convinced it was twins. I was so sick but never threw up.

At the ultrasound, it was confirmed that it was a single pregnancy. I saw Luke breathe again. He was nervous about this second baby. He was such a good Dad but he had a hard time with the adjustment. He is so devoted, that having too many things in his life at once stretched him thin. With dogs, a cat, a baby and me, and himself, I felt he was close to the edge, about to fall off. He was sometimes distant and I took that to mean he didn't want to be there.

I thought he might leave.

After Lily was born I felt the physical strains of the birth took my muscle and my strength, but then I realized it was only temporary. Having Lily actually made me stronger, not just my body but my power. I felt powerful as a mother. I felt strong and that I would do anything for my children. I felt more me than ever before and I felt I could start to express it and live it.

As the baby inside me grew and my belly grew much faster this time, I was feeling uneasy about how Luke felt about our life. I wondered if it was my voices taking me in old dead-end directions or if my intuition was speaking to me.

Feeling the tension within me, I asked Luke if we could talk. I put Lily in her crib earlier and she was sleeping. We walked in the kitchen and leaned on the counters opposite each other. It felt awkward not to reach for him, in my past needy ways, but I didn't. I stood.

I knew I had to ask the question if not just to clear the air but for my own empowerment moving forward in the direction of motherhood and what it held for us all.

"I feel you're tense about having another baby. It makes me nervous to see you this way because I take it personally. I want to fix it and I know it's not something I can fix. I'm excited about our new baby and our growing family. Is this something you want too or do you want to leave and not be with us anymore?"

Silence.

My mind started moving. I said it.

Saying that to Luke was one of the hardest things I've

ever done and it was the choice I was willing to make to guide our children in a truthful, loving and courageous life. I didn't want to be with him if he didn't want to be with us. I could feel his love for us and I could feel him being scared too. We looked at each other.

"I don't want to leave you all. It's a lot though."

"I know and I know we can do this if we talk to each other and just take it one step at a time. This is a huge change in our life but I think we're ready, do you."

"Yes," he said. We hugged.

"I love you."

"I love you too."

Emma was born on May 6, 2003 by a natural birth. After having a C-section, I experimented with something different for my pregnancy. I walked and did yoga only for my exercise. I also had a baby to take care of while pregnant with Emma. Lily kept me busy and we had outings together every day. She crawled, walked and talked early on. She was always on the move and curious. My parents said she was a lot like me; I had walked at six months and talked at nine months. Lily was crawling at six and walking at ten months. She was determined to move forward and start her life with courage.

I amped up my yoga practice. Baron Baptiste, one of my favorite teachers was teaching a workshop in Jacksonville, Florida about an hour from St. Simons Island, Georgia and I was excited to go. My friend Annie and I were going for the day.

During the workshop, Baron stopped to teach handstand in more detail from the front of the room. I knew he was going to ask for a volunteer. Already, my throat got the weird lump in it, my heart started racing and I felt the voice in my heart say "raise your hand and go." Baron asked for a volunteer. I raised my hand with a dozen more people. He pointed to me and said "come on up."

Shit, did I just do raise my hand?

Yes, I did.

As he talked through the alignment of handstand, I moved into the posture with his guidance. I felt safe and tentatively on edge at the same time. I was nervous. Could I hold this handstand in front of 100 plus people? This was not my strong pose.

I was feeling uncertain and weak. I focused on the sound of my deep oujaii breath to drown out the voices in my head which had started to shred the moment with their usual criticisms. My calming oujaii breath, Baron's voice, and supportive assist invited and empowered me to stay in handstand.

There was more. I continued to focus on breath and the centering voice in my heart. I felt the transcendence of trust of something bigger than I was. I felt the power of God within my heart and I knew. I knew there was purpose beyond this handstand but that this pose was teaching me in this very moment. In a millisecond of this moment, I smiled with my eyes and heart in recognition of this acceptance and realization.

I received the breath of life and slowly lowered out of handstand and into child's pose. As I bowed in child's pose and Baron continued to teach, tears of thankfulness pooled in my eyes.

I walked out of the workshop room and looked right. There it was. An advertisement for an intensive Yoga Life Coaching Training with Debbie Williamson. It practically jumped into my hands.

That was it.

My next step.

How was this going to happen? I was not in my best financial state to pay for a training and travel in Costa Rica. I didn't want to ask Dad. He had done so much for me.

I told Mom about it and she mentioned that Uncle Turner had set up a family foundation for continuing education for the nieces, nephews, and grandchildren.

Uncle Turner was actually my great uncle and was my granddaddy's brother. He was Dad's uncle. He never married and he loved that he had so much extended family children. He always mailed a birthday card to all of us with a check for $100 and he never forgot a birthday.

I decided to call Uncle Turner and ask what I needed to do to apply for continuing education financing for my coaching training being held in Costa Rica. I was a little nervous to ask; there was still a part of me that thought I should be able to do this on my own and not ask for help.

I had to get up my courage and just talk to him. What's the worst that could happen?

I went to my office desk, sat down with all the training information in front of me. "Cammie, I'm so happy to talk to you. How are Luke and the girls? Are you still loving St. Simons Island?"

I loved talking to him. Just like my grandparents, his interest in my life was genuine and uninterrupted by texting or another call. He really wanted to know. I told him we were all great and the kids were growing like crazy. He said he enjoyed the photos I sent and he loved seeing how much the girls were looking like Luke and me.

Breathe.

Swallow.

Sit tall.

Ask.

"Uncle Turner, I wanted to ask you about the foundation you established to help the kids in the family who wanted to move forward with continuing education? I have a coaching training that I would like to attend. It's in Costa Rica. It would be an awesome addition to my private yoga business.

"I feel like I've already been coaching informally in my private training with clients. I would love to learn more and I know I can add more value to my clients' lives by becoming a certified coach. It's interesting because I think I'm meant to do this because for so long in my life people I meet tell me things and then say, "you're so easy to talk with, I've never shared that with anyone. I believe I can hone in on this gift with this intense training and help a lot of people."

Breathe.

Relax your body.

Listen.

"Cammie, that sounds incredibly interesting and valuable for you not just in your business but in your life with Luke and the girls growing up too. The foundation is no longer active but I would like to personally fund your training and your trip for you."

My heart jolted. It was really happening.

"This is going to be a magnificent experience for you Cammie and I'm happy I can do this for you. You go ahead and commit to the training and I'll send you a check today."

Tears and immense amounts of gratitude rose from my heart, to my throat and formed the words,

"Thank you Uncle Turner, this means so much to me. I am so ready. Thank you."

I mattered.

I was recognized.

I felt validated.

I was going to Costa Rica for my life coach training.

Breathe.

Trust.

Listen.

Go.

I didn't know anyone going on the trip to Costa Rica for the Yoga Life Coach Training. At baggage claim, I asked a woman if she was in Costa Rica for a yoga retreat.

"Yes, I'm here for my Yoga Life Coach Certification Training."

"Me, too", I said.

We spotted the van from Pura Vida and climbed aboard for the scenic ride to the retreat center, windy roads through town, kids playing outside small colorful homes, up the hill, dogs and chickens scurrying along the road, roosters flapping their wings and doodling as we climbed the hill to our destination.

I checked in at the front desk and they showed me to my room where I met my roommate Melanie. How funny, she lived in Jacksonville, Florida just an hour from where I lived in St. Simons Island. There were several of them she said from a Baptiste affiliated studio, M Body. So excited to meet them and learn about their studio.

That night we all met and got to know each other with a yoga class and then dinner. There were twenty six of us there for the retreat, not all would be involved in the in-depth intensive for the life coach training. I went to bed feeling hopeful, grateful, and accomplished. Tomorrow we would start with our training.

It all begins. Debbie asked us to sit in a circle so we could see everyone's faces and be able to make eye contact with each person. I was ready to learn to be a coach. I was excited and showed up with my usual self, organized, good spot to sit in, and observing all who walked in the room with a smile to greet them and some guardedness which always accompanied me.

I got this.

Look confident and act as if you know what you are doing.

These thoughts were always with me. I just felt better if I kept a little distance. I didn't want to get to close to anything in case I needed a quick getaway or to change my mind about something or someone. It was my protection not to let things get to close. Important to keep my orbit around me big enough so people didn't get too close or know too much. Not sure what they would think about me. I could do it very well without hurting anyone. I didn't want to hurt anyone's feelings and I needed to feel safe.

"We're going to go around the circle, please share your name, where you're from, what you do and why you're here." Watching each person carefully, I do my best to remember their names and I'm especially interested in why they're here. How much do I share on that? Should I tell the real reason that this was a sign or just keep it more surface and don't take the risk yet? My heart was pounding and racing as it came closer to my time to speak. I felt the lump in my throat. "I'm Camden Hoch. I live in St. Simons Island, Georgia. I'm a yoga instructor and also work with a network marketing company sharing health products. I'm here because I've been technically coaching with clients since I became involved in fitness teaching aerobics and personal training in the early 90's. People often comment they tell me things they've never been comfortable telling anyone. They say they trust me and find wisdom in what I have to share with them. So I'm here to get formal training and to learn more so I can help more people."

It came out faster than I planned and I don't think I took a breath. That's it.

Stop there my voices say. That's enough for now.

My lump begins to retreat. I'm done. Breathe.

I may have been led here but I still needed to maintain some control within the threads of trusting the sign.

Done with our names, Debbie laid out what was expected of each of us to successfully complete the training and how we would follow up in our continuation after leaving Costa Rica. She also explicitly stated that whatever was shared within this group would stay within this group. We were expected to be honest, encouraging, and supportive of each person in the group, complete our assignments, and come 100% ready to each part of the training. She sounded strict and at first, I felt restricted and confined but after thinking about what she said that evening, it all seemed right. We had to be present, give and receive and be willing to play by the rules to get the most from this training. There was no messing around. She was direct. I liked that.

It reminded me of Sabine and I recognized the strength in being direct and clear. It made it easier to know how to respond.

No bullshit.

As I knew it would, the meditation and daily yoga practices cracked us open. Wasn't that purposeful. Break us open and fill us up. The practice points out or reflects with such precision that thing within each of us that is ready to break open. Has not failed since I started practicing. The answers are always inside.

Baron often says, "The mat is your mirror." Your practice shows you where you are showing up and where you are avoiding. I already knew but I didn't want it to come out because I knew it would be messy and I wouldn't look perfect. Shit. Something was coming up and I wasn't sure how to keep it down. I wasn't drinking on this trip. I was practicing a ton of yoga. I was headed for a grand collision.

Debbie said most of us would have a breakthrough on the trip and if not on this trip, it would be shortly after we returned home. I did my best to hold in my feelings about my parent's divorce and now Dad was getting remarried. It happened so fast.

After forty-three years of marriage, how was this happening now. Couldn't Mom and Dad just sit down and talk, get it all out in the open, apologize and decide to move on or work it out. This had been happening for so long in their marriage. From my view, there just wasn't any communication that led to any form of resolution. Things would get mentioned but to me it looked as if they didn't end in a solution but instead were pushed under the rug or in my case shoved in the closet. It seemed so simple for them to talk. Why was I in the middle of this? Was it me bringing this to me? How could I help so there wasn't so much hurt? There was too much to take care of with my parents, Luke and our children too. I was overwhelmed and spread thin. I wanted to help and it wasn't enough. I was failing again. I had to make it right and do my best to help.

The training was incredibly edgy. The practices and meditation were revealing. I missed Luke and the girls. Luke and I agreed we would only talk once while I was gone. He wanted to give me the space to be where I needed to be and he would take care of everything at home.

I talked to him once and it made me mad. He was having dinner with a friend. She was a friend of both of ours. I was jealous. Wasn't I over this stuff yet? Why was I jealous and afraid he would leave me still? I was so over feeling this and it wasn't as bad as it used to be but it wouldn't go away. I still had some work to do.

The voices told me a story where while I was away, Luke was with her. I knew it wasn't true but I was mad and worried. I didn't want to feel this way anymore. How do I get rid of this?

Maybe Debbie will talk about this type of thing one day and I will have the answer. Each day I was moving deeper in my practices and having healing treatments with gifted bodywork therapists. More was stirring inside me and ready to break through.

I could feel the welling up inside me and I cried quiet tears in the shower so no one would hear me. I had to deal with this. What kind of coach breaks down at their own stuff? I was there to learn how to coach others. I should have my own stuff more together.

Debbie had offered each of us a private coaching session with her and mine was scheduled for today. Morning mediation, yoga and breakfast - check. Training time. We gathered in our circle. I had formulated and rehearsed many times in my mind what I would talk to Debbie about. Then she dropped a bomb on us in the training session.

"There is one question that if you're brave enough to ask someone you trust can have the potential to change your life," she said. Every part of me jumped to attention and was quiet. No voices. Silence.

If you want to really know more about yourself and live in a way that makes a positive statement in the world, just ask someone you trust this question, "What is your perception of me?"

Shit. That is big. That is change your life big. Could I do that? If you do it, you're taking a big risk. They might find out that you're really not who you appear to be. My life looked good from the outside but inside there was confusion, fear, clutter, lack, and more lack.

If people knew the real me, they would know that I wasn't perfect, that I wasn't good with money, that I was weak and scared. I couldn't risk it. The voices were sounding off. Yes, and on the other hand, I could come out. I wouldn't have to hide anymore. A big part of me had already been exposed. Now I could let out even more.

I bet I would feel even more relief and would have a handle on who I really was and what was true for me. I was shushing the voices with my heart's reasons for coming clean, even more clean. It was time to tell the truth, not just tell it but live it. I was ready.

I promised myself to ask Debbie the question when we met privately. I felt it in my heart that this was the next step. It was risky and necessary. If I was going to be a good mom to our girls and an effective coach, it was time for me to stand up. If I wanted my marriage to Luke to grow and be strong, then I had to do it. If I wanted to get out of this clutter and set myself free and move my life forward, then I had to do it. If I wanted to build a relationship with myself where I trust and love myself then I had to do it. I don't like to be forced with word "had" but I did have to do it. It was the only choice that would open up parts of me to the light and let go parts of me that were complete and no longer protecting me but only smothering me.

Time to meet with my coach, Debbie. I knew I didn't have to ask the question, but I wanted to. The rebel in me sensed the dare and I was ready. I sat down at the table across from her.

We had a brief exchange and I shared how much I was enjoying the training and that what she shared with us was so powerful. I told her I was going to take her advice and ask the question.

Looking her in the eyes, "I took the question you shared with us to heart and I'm ready to hear what you have to say. What's your perception of me?"

I had my pen in hand ready to take notes. Writing things down and taking great notes helped me absorb on a deeper level what I was hearing. She looked at me, very confident and very clear and said, "On the outside you're beautiful. You appear very confident like you have it all together but on the inside you're scared, your self-esteem is low, you're fragile and you're limiting yourself. In this training you say just enough to stay safe. You don't get too involved because you're afraid of not looking perfect. You come across as being better than and yet it distances you from the group. You're afraid to be vulnerable because you don't want to lose control."

Tears rolling down my face. Tears of relief that she saw me and tears of sadness because I was sad that the person she saw was inside me. I had been sad for a long time. I had carried the trophy of pain with me as a reminder of what I had not been able to fix.

I hadn't been able to fix Mom's drinking. I hadn't been able to fix my family. I hadn't been able to fix my parent's marriage. I hadn't been able to forgive myself. I hadn't been able to love myself because I didn't feel worthy.

So much about me was wrong and my "wrongness" was my burden.

Rebirth

Nothing can be forced, receptivity is everything.

B.K.S. Iyengar

After being up most of the night

hearing them yell and argue, I woke up that summer morning July 26th, 1986 and walked out to the den to see her up drinking coffee and watching Good Morning America. I was surprised to see her awake after last night. She looked up from her coffee mug and I saw it.

I understood from the look in her eye that something had shifted. The conflict had forced a change and a decision.

I asked her if she was ready to go yet. She hid her tears and her face. I understood her sadness, fear, guilt and shame. She said she was ready. I knew I didn't have it in me to do this alone, so I called one of her best friends.

She said we better hurry and go this morning before she changed her mind. I could see the fatigue and worry in her face. I also knew she was hungover and at her bottom.

It was time.

I'd been hoping and praying for this change and here it

was. I wasn't sure what it all meant yet but I knew it was a step forward in a new direction toward healing and I also knew that none of us could live this way anymore. It was time to let go.

It's time to let go.

On the weekends, I would go to the nun's house and visit them. St. Mary's was walking distance from my house and most days I walked to and from school. You could say the nuns lived in my neighborhood.

They lived together in the coolest house with a chapel inside. They would invite me in, share a snack and some juice, and ask if I wanted to go to the chapel. I did sometimes.

They were just like normal people.

When I went to their house, I saw that they gardened, they cooked, and their house was like others, but with a chapel. They wore their habits all the time. They wore navy blue with white. I wondered what they wore underneath if it was a jumpsuit or shorts like we wore under our school uniforms.

My favorite teacher was my 6th grade teacher, Sister Charles. At Christmas, I wanted get her a gift and I wasn't sure what to get a nun for Christmas. Mom and I talked about it and we decided on rose soap.

I took the gift to her home and watched her open it. I'm not sure who was smiling bigger when she opened the gift. It made me so happy that she was pleased and I knew she would enjoy her gift.

Enjoy the gift.

There's a surrender that happens when you ride a horse. It's a relationship. It's not like driving a car. There's an understanding that happens between the horse and rider that requires respect, humility, strength, and a deep continuous listening to the layers of the experience.

The power, beauty, grace, and majesty of my horses, Fat Pat and George, connected me to these qualities within me. They turned on the power switch and surges of each of these characteristics started to come alive not only when I rode but began to seep into all parts of my life.

I began to think differently. I made decisions that changed the direction of my life, like not compromising myself in a marriage that was a dead end for me. I left the Hill and left my husband. I became a certified fitness instructor and personal trainer, because I loved it.

That's one of the greatest perks about the roadmap is that we all meet people and yes, animals too, that give us guidance into deeper parts of ourselves. People may say a word or share an experience that awakens a dormant dream or gives a clue to the next step you're to take in your life.

Fat Pat, through his love, acceptance, and guidance, gave me the courage to take a risk, and the acceptance and humility to receive it and live from this place of trust, whether it was jumping my first course in a horse show, staring a new job, or leaving my marriage. The choice was mine and so were the consequences. It was my life to live not anyone else's.

I was learning a new way.

I was taking a new road.

Take a new road.

In Truth Lies Wisdom & Freedom: The meaning of these words was my inspiration for my new tattoo for my birthday this year. For me, tattoos are a representation of stages of integration in my life. It's an interesting process of knowing where the tattoo will show up, what it will be, and the impression it has on how I live my life after it's become of part of my embodiment of life.

About a year ago I started to feel the energy of the tattoo on my body and I knew I wanted to be able to see it every day when it was on my body. I have some on my back and I don't see them but I know they're there and they inspire me in different ways than the tattoos I see every day.

I kept feeling the tattoo and that it was becoming a part of me and was an opening to something that was ready to be seen and heard in my life and it was inviting me to step through a portal in my life. This meant letting go and completing some old patterns and stories.

I knew the tattoo would be a bird but I wasn't sure which bird or would it be flying, perching, or what? I began looking through sketches, researching meanings of birds and looking to nature in her wisdom to guide me.

Time passed and Luke and I flew to Los Angeles from Sausalito in February 2015 to meet Mark at Mark Mahoney's Shamrock Social Club. Mark has been tattooing me for almost ten years. He is gifted, intuitive, and the most incredible artist!

After lunch at the Sunset Towers, Luke and I sat by the pool, ordered ice cream sundaes, and I started looking online for sketches. I completely trusted the process, and Mark, and knew all would come together. I had picked the bird, but it didn't quite have the look.

Then I found it. A chickadee. It symbolizes truth and wisdom. I found the perfect little chickadee flying with purpose, beauty, and intention.

Luke and I caught a cab to meet Mark. We greeted, and hugged, and headed to the back room for our experience. Mark asked where I wanted my tattoo; we decided on size and the perfect placement so I could see my birdy each day and be reminded of this time in my life and its meaning.

I was giddy and ready for the commitment and adventure. A tattoo is a commitment, just like any decision in life.

Own it.

Embody it.

Wear, speak, live, and honor its symbolism and meaning.

I am happy to share with you, my little chickadee...

Radiance Living

You can overcome anything that seems insurmountable. I stand for you, wherever you are, to live as who you are, in your radiance, your most beautiful expression of your soul.

Camden Hoch

Preparing dinner one night, and chatting with Luke, I shared with him that I felt different. Something inside me had changed and was still changing.

"Do I look different?" I asked him. "My body feels different. My being feels different. My soul feels different and I'm not sure how to even describe it yet. Let me get back to you because I want to find the best words to describe it to you" I said.

He jokingly smiled and said, "Maybe you've been through a shift."

This was a joke between us. I shift a lot. I am a truth seeker. I go deep inside. I meditate. I ask God for answers, wait, and feel them through my intuition.

Luke is used to my shifts by now but we still have a giggle about it. He calls me a Life Poet and I agree adding

145

that I'm a shape shifter. It's the evolution of my life. It's the evolution of LIFE.

That same week, I met with my life coach on the phone. I told her the same thing, but I hadn't put my finger on what it was. Rather than controlling it and having to know the answer, I was waiting. I knew it would come. Now I have more trust and I know it always does and most times when I'm not looking for it.

Breathe.

Let go.

Trust.

Luke and I went away to Indian Springs in Calistoga, California for a few days to focus on us, to be intimate, be silly, and be in the essence of our love. I still couldn't put my finger on it but again, I was feeling this feeling. I felt more confident in my skin. I felt more at home inside myself. I felt more me.

I felt lighter.

I felt a piece of me had been put back together.

I felt whole.

When I was younger living in extremes, holding on to the darkness became normal for me. I had a close friend in high school that shot himself because he was ashamed of bringing home bad grades again. That's what everyone said when we found out he shot himself. He had been kicked out of one boarding school and Darlington was his last chance. He couldn't go through the pain of telling his parents and feeling their disappointment. He couldn't live through it. It was easier to end it all.

I get it.

I thought that too many times.

I had suicide ideation. I had no idea it had a name.

Not everyone has these thoughts?

I've always thought that killing myself was an option if it got too bad. I was good at knowing my options. Being the daughter of a lawyer, I made my case well and I learned how to argue my case at a young age.

When I asked Dad or Mom to do something, I had several options worked out, at least A through E. I would figure it out. That's me. Figure out the pieces and how they all fit. Make it nice and neat and it's all done.

Control worked well for me as I tried to control my life. And then it didn't. It was out of control. There was one option that I always knew I had if the pain was unmanageable. Suicide. I could stop the pain myself. I didn't trust God or anyone else. I couldn't share my secrets or struggle. I was ashamed. I hid it well. I was in control or so I thought. If no one ever liked me again or thought I was pretty, I didn't have to be here anymore. If anyone found out about the rapes and thought I was bad and disgusting, I didn't have to be here anymore.

If I was abandoned and alone, I didn't have to be here anymore.

If my parents grounded me again and I didn't get what I wanted, I didn't have to be here anymore.

If I ran out of money because I was dumb and couldn't manage it, I didn't have to be here anymore.

If I couldn't get a hold of my life and do what I was supposed to do, I could kill myself.

Suicide was always on my list of untold options visible to me but invisible and unspoken to anyone else. By blindly thinking I was managing my pain and trauma, I was slowly killing myself with addictions and distractions of alcohol, drugs and whatever else kept me temporarily anesthetized and pushed the pain down so I didn't have to look at it or feel it. When the anxiety, sadness, depression or pain would come up and brutally remind me of my faults, I would push it down further. I didn't even want to look in the mirror. I couldn't see anyway. Emptiness was looking back at me through my own eyes.

Who is that?

Who am I?

In 2009, living in St. Simons Island after my failed suicide plan, I told Luke what happened on the closet floor. I wanted to kill myself because I was ashamed and a failure.

"It would solve everything," I told him. "You would get the insurance money because I would make it look like a natural death and I would be gone and wouldn't cause you and the girls any more pain or embarrassment."

He was shocked at what just came out of my mouth. He couldn't believe my words.

"Why would you ever say that?" his words leaped from his mouth in a strong and "are you crazy" tone.

I was shocked that he was shocked.

I thought to myself, *Had he never thought of killing himself before?* I thought it was normal. I saw from the reaction on his face that not everyone saw suicide as a solution.

I felt ashamed.

His voice softened and his eyes locked on mine, "I would never want you to do that Camden, ever."

I used to think I was crazy with the voices talking to me, my extreme shifts from good girl to combusting while drinking too much, or high, and letting it all go. I was exhausted from trying to manage my pain. I didn't know how to let go. When I drank, or was high, it was fun.

Then it wasn't.

It exposed me. It exposed me to myself that I wasn't living my truth. It was buried in my trauma. When I combusted, it all came out. I couldn't live like this. I couldn't do this to Lily and Emma. I didn't want to pass this on to them and I didn't want them to experience anything like this.

At times, it hasn't even been easy writing this book because the writing took me back into the pain that was unhealed. It had to and I chose to go, unknowingly at first, because I didn't realize I needed to go so deep to find this lost part of my self. My companion of suicidal thoughts had traveled with me so far, for so long.

All my experiences and all of the people who have touched my life in varied ways have been a part of this twisting and turning roadmap of my life that has led me into the gifts of my true nature which is radiance.

It was always there and now I'm home.

I'm home in my body and soul.

This was it, the change I mentioned to Luke. I didn't feel that darkness looming. I didn't feel the suicidal option anymore. I felt free. I had seriously considered suicide; and tried but failed. I acknowledge my deep secrets. I am free. They don't hold me.

The voices have no blackmail power over me any longer. I feel joy. I am different inside and out. I don't think of suicide anymore as an option, and haven't for a while.

I have faith in being Divinely led in my life. I trust even in the unknown. I know the darkness and it knows me. Because of this I now see the light even more clearly. Even in the darkest days, the light was still calling me. Because of seeing death clearly, I am now living.

I am radiance living.

Camden Hoch

A Gift from Camden

Thank you so much for purchasing

and reading my book, *Roadmap To Radiance.*

I'm happy to offer you this complimentary gift of my guided meditations which I personally recorded for you. They are a perfect accompaniment to reading my book and for your life anytime, anywhere, for focus and calm.

Please go to the link provided here to receive your meditations for download which you will have to listen to at any time.

http://camdenhoch.com/guided-meditation-free-gift/

To learn more about Camden Hoch, please visit www.camdenhoch.com

Sending you much love and happy adventures,

Camden

Camden Hoch

About the Author

Author, speaker, life coach, yogini, wife, and mom, Camden Hoch has helped hundreds of people re-imagine what is possible in their lives with her Radiance Living Program. Roadmap To Radiance is her first book. Her life as a spiritual adventure has been a journey in both dark and light,  extreme living, and transformed to a life of love, purpose, prosperity, and service of others.

She lives in Sausalito, California, with her daughters, Lily and Emma, and her husband, Luke, plus their furry children.

56921431R00102

Made in the USA
Charleston, SC
03 June 2016